A GLIMPSE
OF DAVID

A GLIMPSE OF DAVID

AN ORDINARY MAN WITH AN EXTRAORDINARY GOD

Selected poems, prose, psalms and prophecy by

DAVID CHALUISAN, JR.

collected by the Chaluisan family

A Glimpse of David

ISBN-13: 978-1533330185

ISBN-10: 1533330182

First Edition: April 1, 2016

10 9 8 7 6 5 4 3 2 1

DEDICATION

"Where, O death, is your victory? Where, O death, is your sting?""
1 Corinthians 15:55

This book is dedicated to those young men whom the Lord has commissioned and anointed to spread the Gospel of Christ. This call is not without a price as their lives bear the scars of a life poured out to bring the message of hope to a dying world. When Adam and Eve walked in the Garden of Eden they were created without blemish or sin's tarnish. They were created specifically in the image of God the Father, but when they disobeyed God by eating of the forbidden fruit of the Tree of Knowledge – they became tainted and sin made its entrance. This disobedience would bring about permanent separation from God because a Holy God is unable to be in the presence of sin. Even then, our God had a plan! A plan to reconcile us back to our home -- a true demonstration -- of His love for us.

In enters our Creator and Father. He who was sinless and holy would become our Advocate in the form of Jesus Christ the Son and come down in the flesh to rescue us. Centuries later this same message – one with eternal ramifications – is still being conveyed by God's servants. These chosen vessels were not picked due to their perfect lives or external appearances – no, the opposite was true, the only prerequisite was obedience to the call of a perfect God!

FOREWORD

"Does the LORD delight in burnt offerings and sacrifices as much as in obeying the LORD?
To obey is better than sacrifice." --1 Samuel 15:22

"God's got an army not afraid to fight -- soldiers of the cross, children of the light, warriors of righteousness with healing in their hands."

My uncle, David Chaluisan Jr., always had some kind of Christian music playing in his room, and Carman was one of his favorites. I remember most of the words to several songs almost 20 years later despite not hearing them since his passing. The example he set was so indelible it charted my course through adulthood.

My uncle didn't just profess the name of the Lord on Sunday and live like a heathen the remainder of the week. His daily life was a testimony of how a regular guy can follow the example of some words in a 2,000 year old book. Jesus wasn't just some Sunday school teaching to him. God was someone you could talk to, thank, lean on, and worship every day. It changed my life to see an example of how Christianity can be lived practically even in today's world. I guess in that respect, the Word was literally brought to life.

David Chaluisan Jr. is just a name on page to you at this time. I pray by the time you close this book, you will see "a glimpse" of Dave. While Carman's song was the first to tell me God is not afraid to fight, my Uncle showed me what that fight looked like Now, let me introduce you to the man I knew as Uncle David.

-- Danny Jr.

CONTENTS

INTRODUCTION

For you have need of endurance, so that after you have done the will of God, you may receive the promise." – Hebrews 10:36

Reverend David Chaluisan, Jr. was 28 years old when the Lord called him home. With much time spent seeking God's direction, we set out to compile David's writings in book form. *A Glimpse of David* is a compilation of our brother, uncle, and cousin, Reverend David Chaluisan, Jr.'s, written work. Within these pages are poems, letters, personal journals, prophetic writings and excerpts from books he hoped to complete. We knew shortly after David's death that his desires had now become our desire, not to pay homage to a man, but to magnify the extraordinary God of this ordinary man!

We chose to precede each chapter with a brief glimpse of David's life, narrated by one of his loved ones, to introduce you to this ordinary man with an extraordinary God. Since David measured everything against the Word of God, the scripture passages included in each chapter denote that important fact. Other scriptures are referenced by the narrators to introduce a chapter or a particular subject.

To preserve the integrity and style of David's written work, we present it here with very slight edits. As you read through these simple, yet sincere writings, our goal and prayer is for all who read this book to yearn for the same relationship David enjoyed and cultivated with the Lord. His intentions were to never condemn or judge anyone in his writing, but rather to communicate a clear-cut message about his Creator.

David was learned in all the world's religions and was ready to discuss or debate his faith in love, but with conviction. David had a convincing way of always linking his conversation back to God's infallible word, the Bible, for answers. His mission was for all to experience the same unconditional love and peace he had encountered at the cross through Christ's saving grace. As a man of God, he spoke the truth from God's word, always in love, but without sugar coating it.

David's ordinary life will not point you to the many churches this young pastor planted or the various countries he visited. Nor will you read about the award-winning books he published and the seminary degrees he earned.

No, that will not be written in these pages, bec ause none of those things occurred during David's time here. What you will read about is how this ordinary young man was consumed by an extraordinary God, directly resulting in a lifelong pursuit for his Savior!

David never married, but had many friendships with his brothers and sisters in Christ. Never having any children of his own, David passed on his love for God and his knowledge of God's Word to his nieces and nephews. He made it a point to pour into them by reading and teaching them the Word, and spoke to them of God's amazing love. The seeds he planted will remain with them forever because they are rooted in Christ; not in David's life or death, but in the Savior!

The children had a special bond and love for their Uncle David. After David's passing we learned that he had shared many dreams and goals with them which we were not aware of. The wisdom he imparted from God's Word and his relationship with Christ is evident through these stories. Despite some detours, the seeds he planted in these young men and women will remain forever and will affect them for Christ! When David was called home, a void was left in their hearts, both spiritually and emotionally, for their beloved Uncle David. It was heartbreaking to watch and even more so to try and explain why he was now gone. His passing changed their lives forever.

Compiling David's written work was not an easy task and at times an emotional roller coaster. Some days were filled with joy as we gleaned words of wisdom from every line and page, but other days just a glance at the page would bring tears. Losing David so suddenly and in the prime of his life was and remains difficult to understand. But we are blessed, not only with the indelible mark he left within our family, but because he entrusted us with a precious piece of himself through his written work and audio sermons. We prayerfully felt we had to make one of the two decisions: either keep them to ourselves as our gift or share this gift --- with the latter being David's desire.

Perhaps most importantly, if you're reading these words, it was God's desire! When King David was about to die he told his son, Solomon: "Be strong and show yourself a man; keep the charge of the Lord God, walk in His ways, keep His statues, His commandments, His precepts, and His testimonies, as it is written in the Law of Moses, that you may do wisely and prosper in all that you do and wherever you turn" (1 Kings 2:1-7.)

Our brother's life, and especially his death, caused us to take personal inventory of our walk with the Lord. We pray David's written work and his testimony will cause you to reflect as well. As we depart this life, what we leave behind will be our "Legacy." What will your Legacy resemble? The choice is ultimately yours.

CHAPTER ONE

<u>HOMECOMING</u>

It was Sunday, March 24, 1996 at 10:30 pm, and we were sitting around the table finishing up a very late dinner. Then I heard the phone ring.

I thought, "It can't be Mom..." because I had spoken to her early that evening and all was well in Florida. As the phone rang again, we heard my brother-in -law, Mark, begin to leave a message on the machine. Danny Jr., my oldest, ran to pick up the receiver. Most families would find it strange to receive calls this late in the evening, but not our family; this was standard practice for us.

Except this time. This one was different. There was something wrong, and I sensed it in the pit of my stomach. I began to cry when my son handed the phone to my husband as his uncle had requested. As my husband walked toward the bedroom to speak to Mark in private, the boys and I anxiously awaited his return, but could never imagine the heartbreak that awaited us. Not being able to contain it any longer, I found myself running to the bedroom to ask him what was happening. Seconds seemed like hours as I waited for my husband to hang up the phone.

Something terrible had happened, my husband explained. His words echoed in my head, never to be forgotten. He said, "They tried to wake him, and could not." As I screamed in horror, I asked "Who?!" Automatically assuming it was my father, I said, "No, not my dad, please!"

He said, "No, not your dad. Your brother."

I heard him, but could not comprehend his words.

Once again, I attempted to find out what my husband was trying to say and I asked him, "What are you talking about? David?! Lord, not David!"

I have never known such pain and utter helplessness as I experienced that never-ending night. Danny went on to tell me that David was dead, and Dad was in the hospital. When my father, mother and sister Becky discovered David in his bed, Dad suffered an angina attack and was in the hospital being monitored, as a precaution.

As I cried, I thought, "Oh Lord, Why?" I asked God to please wake me from this horrible nightmare and tell me everything was all right. Except as surreal as all this seemed, unfortunately it was really happening.

I could not believe David was gone so suddenly --- and possibly my father was about to be taken from my family as well? I thought of my family in Florida and the hundreds of miles that separated us. I cried for the agony and pain they had experienced in finding David and trying desperately to awaken him from his sleep.

Would my family be able to survive this?

I longed to be by their side and reassure them we would get through this, not really knowing that we could, wishing the distance that separated New York and Florida to simply disappear.

I vividly remember my boys sitting on the bed beside their father as he desperately tried to both comfort and explain that their uncle was gone. As their young faces filled with tears, I realized their innocence had collided with the finality of death and they could not understand what was happening. This same scene was recreated in my sister's home that tragic evening as she tried to explain what had happened to my niece and nephew.

As I walked around the house sobbing and searching for any remembrance of my brother, I tried desperately to remember his face and feared that would soon be forgotten. That evening, my son Joshua and I laid on the couch together as we held on to the Bible for dear life. We were unable to focus on any particular scripture, but asked the Lord for a word in this tragic situation that was unfolding. As we both fell asleep on the couch, I was certain that when we awoke this whole evening would be nothing but a horrible nightmare.

It was not.

We later learned that David had gone to bed that morning shortly after working the night shift for a local closet manufacturing company. Mom told us he had something to eat and then went to bed, waking up briefly in the afternoon and returning to bed. Later that evening, about 9:30 pm, Mom went to wake him because she noticed the time and figured he had overslept. As she tried waking him, he would not move.

When the ambulance arrived it was too late. David was gone. All the paramedics could do was call the coroner's office. We requested an autopsy and it revealed the contributing factor was dilated cardiomyopathy, a form of congestive heart failure which can result in death. David went to sleep that evening and passed from earth to heaven.

A couple of months prior to his death, David had undergone a physical and received a clean bill of health. The only pre-existing condition we were aware of was his with Rheumatoid Arthritis which he had suffered with since his teenage years. Shortly after David's death we began reading some of his many journals and writings, and we became aware that he had suffered silently for many years with his bout with rheumatoid arthritis. We still do not believe Dave knew that he had heart disease and I'm sure he associated all his symptoms with the rheumatoid condition.

As we mourned David's passing we were faced with many hurdles as a family going through the grieving process – with acceptance of his death being the greatest. In retrospect, all through this difficult process, we were able to see how God was preparing us and assuring us that David was in better hands and his work had been entrusted to us.

We were always aware of David's passion for writing and his immense love for God, but unaware of the treasure he left behind. This treasure overflowed from a lifetime of intimacy with the One he lived for daily. Sadly, we were also reminded of his silent suffering, as referenced through his writings and his constant battle with pain and the weakness that overcame his body. We were reminded how David was diagnosed with Rheumatoid Arthritis at an early age, and this never slowed his pace in serving the Lord, at work and playing the sport he loved, baseball. This was his favorite pastime and there was only room for one team in his heart, the New York Mets. This love stemmed from Dad, who was a die-hard Brooklyn-Dodgers-turned-Mets fanatic.

Discovering all of David's writings was bittersweet, as we now had a tangible part of him entrusted to us in his absence -- this was such a gift! However, we felt as though we only came to fully know his heart upon his passing. Our siblings are an extension of who we are, and as much as we think we know them, it does not compare to the intimate connection provided by reading someone's written expressions of their heart.

We grieved for Dave and for not having the ability to tell him how he inspired us to be more diligent in seeking after God's heart. David's relationship with the Lord is the reason most of his siblings, brother-in-laws, nieces, nephews and many relatives came to know Christ as Savior – both through his life and continuing after his death. As a young boy, David struggled with the destructive forces of anger, lack of self-control, and depression, but once he discovered freedom from these forces through his relationship with Christ, he longed for all to experience that same freedom. After God's transformation, David's peaceful demeanor and patience were a by-product of going through the fire of God's testing and aligning his will with God's.

You see, Jesus took this baby boy, born prematurely after his sister was tragically killed. A young boy raised in the rough streets of Brooklyn, a young boy with unresolved anger, a young boy with failing health and unfulfilled dreams. Jesus reached down and captured this young boy's heart!

The transformation process was a result of many wrestling matches with God, hence David realizing that obedience was all God required; the how's, why's and when's were all mere details. Out of David's obedience came deliverance and God was able to take David's short life-span and give him a full- life in Christ!

David struggled with health issues since his birth and developed scarlet fever when he was seven years old. Scarlet fever caused other health issues in his body including extreme weakness and these issues took a toll on David and affected his emotional state as well as the physical. He developed issues with anger, depression and low self-esteem because of these lingering health problems. He nearly hemorrhaged due to a diseased tonsil, also around aged seven. Thankfully, it happened before Dad left for his overnight shift and he rushed Dave to the emergency room.

In David's later years, the Lord spoke to David and reminded him how he spared his life that evening. The Lord said, Had your father gone to work that evening, you would have died, David.

When he was 11 years old, David attended a church viewing of a movie depicting the end of the world. When the Pastor gave an altar call and asked those that wanted to accept Christ to come up, David hesitated in going to the front, but silently at his seat whispered a prayer that would change his heart forever. The Presbyterian Church was called La Mision (The Mission), located in Williamsburg, Brooklyn. My grandparents were members of La Mision and my parents attended on the holidays and various other times. Mom was raised Catholic and our father knew the Lord, but was not serving Him at the time.

David began to suffer from the physical and emotional effects of his illness, having been diagnosed shortly after dedicating his life to Christ. Shortly, David forgot about his commitment to the Lord for various reasons: physical pain, circumstances, peer pressure, etc. and wrestled with the destructive emotions he thought he had surrendered to the Lord.

When David was in his early teens, our family relocated to Cypress Hills, which sits right on the border of Queens and Brooklyn. David began attending St. Peter's Lutheran Church with a few of his neighborhood friends. That church became a vehicle the Lord would use to keep these teenage boys involved in the church and away from the streets. During those years at St. Peter's, David became a sponge for God's word and fell in love with the scriptures and his new found Savior.

David still struggled with shyness, depression, anger, low self-esteem, and loneliness, due to his health and the surrounding peer pressure. David was an honor student and considered himself a geeky type of guy because he excelled in his studies and did not partake in any of the substance abuse that surrounded him in the neighborhood and in school. During his teenage years he began to swerve off the path and dropped out of high school, but later received his GED from another local school.

Steadfastly, the Lord continued to pursue David, and at 15 years old, he dreamt of worldwide catastrophic events that would occur during the end time periods of the Bible; events similar to ones referred to in the book of Revelation. The very same day he encountered this vision, he turned on the television and he heard a pastor preaching the message of Salvation to those that were backslidden. That's when he surrendered to God completely. David knew God had plans for him and he rededicated his life to the Lord right then and there.

He registered for Concordia College and realized the curriculum did not contain the Biblical studies he was pursuing. Of course this was all before the Internet and online classes, so David signed up for correspondence courses (similar to today's online, but through the mail) in Biblical Studies. God's word began to transform his life physically and spiritually. He encountered the living God and so began the journey home. He would never be satisfied with a lukewarm relationship with Jesus, his Savior.

He later began attending Time Square Church in NYC (Reverend David Wilkerson's Church). In 1991, he was ordained in the same church where was was baptized, Calvary Grace Churches of Faith. When David came to understand the "Grace" message, it changed his life and he knew he was called to preach that message. David spent a brief time in a church in Queens, preaching occasionally, until that Church experienced a divide. David left, broken- hearted regarding the events that transpired and abuse of authority within the leadership of that church.

David and his best friend Pedro, along with the small remnant of that church in Queens, started meeting at the local Elk's Lodge. They formed a church called Covenant of Grace Tabernacle. During that time, Dad retired and we all decided to sell the two family houses in Queens and relocate.

My parents and youngest sister Becky moved to Ocala, Florida and my husband and I moved to Long Island. David decided to stay and continue in the ministry and fellowship he loved because in his heart he felt his work here in New York was not complete.

David, now 24, had to find a place to live, but he obeyed God and continued the journey. He decided to spend a brief time with his cousin Danny in New Jersey, who was more like a brother to David growing up. He also spent a brief time with my sisters Agnes and Cindy in Staten Island and with me in Long Island.

Unfortunately, Covenant of Grace Tabernacle closed its doors. David was crushed and shed many tears trying to understand God's plan, even in this. After much time spent in prayer and seeking God for his next steps, David decided to move to Florida with our parents, leaving his beloved city, friends, family, and the ministry that he felt he was called to and what could have been, but was no more. David felt moving to Florida was a matter of obedience. With some trepidation, he continued the last leg of his journey, not knowing that God would call him home two years later.

David attended various churches in the Ocala area, and was blessed as God continued to speak to his heart. David longed to preach again, but for now knew God was leading him through a different road. David visited one particular church in the Ocala area and felt the Lord leading him to lay hands and pray for the Pastor. David was shy, so I'm sure it was difficult to come up to a total stranger and follow God's leading, but he obeyed and the minister was blessed and so was David. We'll never know how that word impacted that man of God, but God knew, and David obeyed.

David also attended the local church my parents were attending at the time. The church was undergoing a rebuilding project. My parents became members and dad volunteered to assist with the many tasks that a rebuilding project entailed. David passed away before the rebuilding project was completed, but the Church was renamed "Wings of Faith" and there is a statue of an eagle with the following scripture in the entrance, "Isaiah 40:31," which coincidently was David's favorite scripture. David had several framed prints of this magnificent bird in his bedroom and I once commented that these birds were quite frightening to have hanging over your bed. David quickly defended their beauty, uniqueness, and symbolisms.

Once David was settled in Ocala, he knew he had to find a job, either temporarily or until God opened up a door for ministry. This was a difficult time for David because he longed to be in New York fellowshipping with his brothers and sisters in the ministry, but he was also encouraged by joining his family in Florida.

David had a great influence on our youngest sister, Becky, and encouraged her to pursue her driver's license, which Becky received after David's passing. Two peas in a pod; that's what they were, and there was nothing he would not have done for his sister. Before David moved to Florida, his sister Marina had relocated to Ocala from Puerto Rico with her 4-year-old daughter, Julie, shortly after her marriage ended. Marina moved out to give David the spare room in Mom and Dad's home.

David enjoyed spending time with his niece Julie, and began to pour into this little girl's life the word of God, and she loved every minute.

During summer vacations, his New York and New Jersey family would come spend summers with him and the family in Ocala, and together they were discovering Florida through the eyes of New Yorkers and loving it.

Now 26 years old, David continued to pray for God's direction. He purchased a new, economical car and applied for a position with a local closet manufacturer, assembling various components for closet organizers. The job was challenging, with long overnight hours, and required maneuvering heavy equipment. David's Rheumatoid Arthritis was causing severe pain throughout his body constantly. He never complained to anyone, but managed his pain silently and in prayer to the One who brought him thus far.

After the wake and burial, a couple of David's co-workers came to visit Mom and Dad. They wanted to discuss David's work ethic and get to know the family of their beloved co-worker. We knew they were curious and were intrigued, and we knew the Lord led them there.

We were all able to spend some time with them and exchange stories. There was a sense of comfort for them and us, especially for my parents. They shared how much they admired his integrity and professionalism and recalled David going to his car for lunch where they knew he was reading his Bible. They were watching his life, and I'm sure David shared his relationship with the Lord.

They were impressed with his performance, his quiet strength and the high volume he produced for his work shift. They mentioned the volume could never be duplicated after David was gone.

David never shared his daily battle with his debilitating disease with his coworkers and frankly, even with his family, but that day we knew it was God who had sustained him. His co-workers were clearly moved. Even in death, David was still affecting people for Christ and they discovered his source was Jesus!

As a man of faith, David's commitment to the Lord did not waver despite his circumstances. He might not have understood God's plan, but he was obedient. David remained a constant reminder to his family of his uncompromising walk. His life demonstrated how Christ can take an ordinary young man who is sold out for Christ and use him to cause his loved ones and those he encountered to seek out that same relationship with the Lord.

As a man of prayer, his quiet strength was sharpened through studying the scriptures and spending time in his prayer closet. As a result, David was able to pour into those he loved and those he ministered to. Similar to the old Gospel song by one of the greatest gospel singers, Mahalia Jackson, David also humbly proclaimed through his life, "I found the answer, I learned to pray."

CHAPTER TWO

<u>A FATHER'S</u>
<u>FAREWELL</u>

Glimpse: Our Dad penned these words the day after David was called home. This short moving sentiment gives us insight into the heart of a father, who despite losing his only son and not fully comprehending the reason, accepted God's Sovereign plan, even in this:

"Dear Son, I wish I could have gone on this trip with you, but the Lord said there was a reservation for only one. He said not to worry for you will be in good hands, that someday we will be together again. You gave us a good 28-1/2 years. We thank you and bless you and love you, eternally grateful to you and God, and the Lord Jesus the Christ. Amen, AMEN!" --- Dad, Mom, Becky and the rest of your loving sisters and family.

Scripture Reference: "For God is our God Forever and ever; he will be our guide even to the end" (Psalm 48:14.)

"The Undiscovered Country"

The undiscovered country is hidden from man.

Far above our natural eyes, it's there, but unknown.

For no ear has heard, no eye has seen,

The fullness of glory that awaits you and me.

For the Glory came down far from above.

He lived among us just for a while,

Then returned up above far past the stars.

For through the Glory which is Christ,

We have discovered in part that we now have,

Some of the undiscovered country living in our hearts.

So, we believe and receive, we accept and obey,

For the glory, who is Christ died in our place.

So we love, because He first loved us.

He showed us true agape love.

Then our spiritual eyes were opened,

And we caught a glimpse of the undiscovered country.

For the fullness will come, when we see him again,

For the heavens will open and we will behold him.

We will see Him as He is full of glory divine.

Then we will weep tears, full of joy,

A joy unspeakable and full of life.

Then in His sight, we'll be awed by His light,

As He tells us, "Beloved, please come in."

Not questioning or mumbling, because we'll be whole!

Our spirit and resurrected body will meet and be home.

Known fully to all, is Jesus Christ our Lord.

Forever we will sing praises, praises so magnificent,

The heavens will echo and thunder through all eternity.

Then the undiscovered country is made known, forever more,

by Jesus Christ, our Lord.

Written by David Chaluisan, Jr.
Title Written 3/31/94; Written 4/13/94 –10/12/94

CHAPTER THREE

BROTHERS IN LOVE, BROTHERS

Glimpse: The words below were taken from a letter David wrote to the editor of the local newspaper in Ocala about a month before he died. He expresses his gratitude to the local community and acknowledges God's providence in the fire that nearly destroyed his home, as well as all his life's work.

"I'm writing concerning the brush fire that sprang up on 64th Avenue Road, off County Road 464 in Silver Springs Shores on January 28th. My house was one of the properties directly in the path of the fire.

As I was arriving home with my parents and sister around 12:30 p.m. I could see the smoke and fire from CR 464. As we made the left on 64th Avenue Road I could see the fire was almost right on top of my house. But as I came to my driveway I could see people in the yard fighting the fire with our hoses and taking water from our pool in buckets and throwing it at the fire. To see that gave me a feeling of peace even though it was scary seeing the fire as it was picked up by the wind going everywhere.

People who didn't even know us came out to help their neighbors.

Everybody was giving a hand. Some kids from the neighborhood ran from house to house warning people about the fire. Some people from the Church of God a block away came to fight the fire in our yard.

A little fire truck was the only one on the scene when we arrived. I saw my neighbor's house was saved from the fire because of the quick response of the firemen.

In the midst of all the doom and gloom we always hear it was good to see some good being lived out. After everything was back to normal, after the fire, we looked around the property and saw how close it really was, maybe 5 to 10 feet away from our house. My father said, "I think there was a wall of angels around the house to stop it right where it did." I agreed with him and we both thanked God for it. We also appreciate the angels from the neighborhood who came out and showed us all, that there's still a lot of good in the world."

Scripture Reference: Ecclesiastes 4:9-10, 1 Corinthians 12:12, 2 Corinthians 10:12, Romans 2:11

Brothers in Love, Brothers in Unity

We the people of God are one.

One in Spirit, one in truth,

So let us stand in unity together.

For when we stand together,

We are mighty through God,

To destroy all the works of hell.

For God has given us mighty weapons.

They are Divine by the Blood of Christ.

So we must stand as one, through prayer,

And the darkness will flee.

For how good and pleasant it is,

When brothers live together in unity.

It's like the morning dew,

It compels us to love one another,

Because of the love we have received from God.

For two are better than one.

If one falls, his friend can pick him up.

For we are one body in Christ,

Though we are different,

We form one body, not of color or race,

But of one mind, the mind of Christ.

There are no classifications or favoritism,

For Christ Jesus our Lord loves all the same.

For by his Blood we have been set free,

Set free from hate, sin and death.

For we must love as Christ loved,

Without condition, but full of Grace.

We must bring forth healing from our prejudice.

Prejudice that has destroyed the work of God,

From flowing more powerful in our midst.

So go forth and heal your church body,
And then your city, state, and nation will recognize your
Unconditional love and they will be healed as well.
The spirits of lies have reigned over our churches long enough.
Learn to love all, despite differences and our appearances.

For we tend to look on the outward, but God tells us to look,
On the inward of a person to really see them.
When we learn to do this, the body will have,
An eternal peace that will cause us to bring the gospel to all!
For Christ Jesus has destroyed the barrier,
And the dividing wall of hostility!

So we are now reconciled and members of God's household.
For God doesn't judge us by external appearances,

But by His Grace.
Now we are all sons of glory.
To Him we are just one living body,
We are brothers in love, brothers in unity.

Written by David Chaluisan, Jr. on 12/31/93, 1/21/94 & 2/21/94

CHAPTER FOUR

I ASKED
IN THAT NAME

Glimpse: David lived with my parents in Queens when he was pursuing his call in the ministry. When my parents decided to retire and relocate to Florida, it was assumed that David and my younger sister Becky would follow, but David decided to stay behind and continue in his ministry. He was an associate Pastor in a church in Queens, but shortly after my parents moved, that church closed its doors and David was left without a ministry and without a home.

At the time his decision to stay in New York did not make sense, but after his death we understood its powerful significance. David continued studying the Word, writing and fellowshipping with his friends. He spent a brief time in all of his sisters' homes, including his cousin Danny, whom he loved like a brother. With them having spent most of their childhood together, Danny was the brother David never had.

The time he spent in our homes with our children and our spouses were difficult for Dave because he felt the loneliness of not being in the ministry and without a home. But God had a plan! David's decision to stay in New York would result in salvation for some of his sisters, their husbands and his beloved nieces and nephews.

Fast forward to the day David was called home. That evening as I spoke to my sister Cindy for the first time since learning of David's death, her voice was in hysterics and barely audible as she cried out, "David came into our homes to pray for us and to bless our homes and we did not even realize it!" The Lord spoke that evening through a sister's cry to enable us to fully understand the impact of David's obedience, in remaining in New York!

Scripture Reference: "Jesus said to them, 'a prophet is not without honor except in his hometown and among his own relatives and in his own household' " (Mark 6:4.)

I Asked in That Name

I asked the Lord for many things that were good for my soul.

My soul rejoiced in God my Savior for the many things that He had done.

I received, because I did not ask amiss.

I asked for wisdom so I could know.

I asked for understanding so I could grow.

I asked for discernment so I could go.

(Go where I had not gone before, or so I thought.)

I thought back to what God said,

"Greater things than these will you do in my Name."

But I was forgetting, what's in that Name.

It's not just history, or stories and games,

No, it's much more than that.

It's power for the weak, strength for the suffering,

Grace for the sinner and that hasn't changed.

It's been almost two thousand years and still it's that Name.

That name is Jesus.

He's the Lamb that was slain, slain to make us free.

Free so we could live to fellowship with Him.

Now He's our Priest our Shepherd and our King.

So I ask in that Name.

Teach me, guide me, lead me,

So that I may dwell in your loving arms forever.

I ask to abide in your tabernacle, so peaceful, and free.

You, Jesus, my Savior, that is your name.

You descended on my behalf, but also ascended far above the heavens for me.

You conquered death and hades,

So that I would not be afraid of leaving this earthly place.

I believe that I'll live, for I'm born again in your name.

For that is your promise for all who believe.

Since I asked in that name, I've never been the same.

For a Kingdom has come, come into my heart.

It will never be shaken, or spoil or fade.

For I have it by your Grace,

So I see you with love, because you careth for me.

So I asked in your name.

How come you displayed so great a love?

That will never be repaid.

So I wonder in awe, how your Grace is so easy for all to attain.

Yet we struggle with pain, trying to change,

Your Grace, all the same.

So we add and we take away on how it should stay,

But completely negate it is better your (God's) way.

I asked and received your spirit of adoption,

Which remains forever in me.

I'm your child today and forever to stay,

Because of your Grace.

So abide and obey,

And everything else will remain.

So believe in your heart,

Christ's abundant assurance.

And you will find peace.

For only He can fill the emptiness that abides deep within.

So I asked in that Name,

And God supplied all my needs.

He gave according to all His riches in Glory,

To you and to me.

Never lose hope in that precious, glorious Name,

For in that Name is the hope of the World.

So when all is done here on earth as well as in heaven;

I'll be able to say "I asked in that Name,"

And I'm forever changed.

So the Good News has come forever,

To dwell in my heart because I asked in that Name!

Written by David Chaluisan, Jr. 8/11/94 in New Jersey

CHAPTER FIVE

<u>THE EAGLE HAS LANDED</u>

Glimpse: The evening my sister and parents found David in his bed, my sister Becky caught a glimpse of a plaque in David's room which he received on his last Christmas with us. Through tear-filled eyes she began to read the words on the plaque, "I bore you on eagles' wings and brought you to Myself." She knew it was a message from her Savior to reassure not only her, but all of us that David was finally home. Our ever compassionate God sends a word in due season at just the precise time. How can we not love a God like that!?

Scripture Reference: Hebrew 11:13-16

Prelude:

These people all died controlled and sustained by their faith, but not having received the tangible fulfillment of God's promises, only having seen it and greeted it from a great distance by faith, and all the while acknowledging and confessing that they were strangers and temporary residents and exiles on the Earth. Now these people who talk as they did show plainly that they are in search of a fatherland. If they had been thinking with remembrance of that country from which they were emigrants, they would have found constant opportunity to return to it. But the truth is that they were yearning for and aspiring to a better and more desirable country, that is, a heavenly country. For that reason God is not ashamed to be called their God, the God of Abraham, Isaac and Jacob, for He has prepared a city for them.

The Eagle Has Landed

I look up to the heavenlies
To see the eagle soaring through the skies.
His presence causes all to look in awe.
His majesty is beyond words.
His face is like flint, set on its course.
His young await his coming to receive their nourishment.
His hunt is life to them.

He stoops his beak downward to his prey.
His wings envelop the heavens.
And as he opens them outward to glide,
Downward he plunges to rugged places.

So he can give his young glory,
He must go to a place that he knows not of.
So when his purpose is fulfilled,
And he has accomplished his duties as a father.
Once again, he soars upward to his position of power,
To declare his influence over the skies.
And as the night falls over the mountain sides,

The shade of the sun sparkles like red fire.

And as his young cry out to him,

Their weariness subsides,

Because his presence gives his young renewed hope and strength.

As the young eagles look to him,

His presence speaks to them without voice or words,

And say, "To whom will you compare me.

Who is my equal in the heavens?

My presence gives you hope and strength,

The nourishment I give you is sufficient."

So as the sun disappears into the night,

All is well in the next.

Your warmth and love tells me my service,

Has been accomplished this day.

For the Eagle has Landed!

Written by David Chaluisan, Jr. 12/5/93 at 12:30am

CHAPTER SIX

WHAT AM I TO DO, LORD?

Glimpse: The day following Dave's death, as the families in New York and New Jersey ran to catch flights to Florida, my parents and sisters already there had the grim task of making funeral arrangements.

My sisters are all exceptional women, but my sister Marina, living in Florida at the time, was faced with managing my father's care in the hospital and ensuring Mom and my younger sister Becky were fine. She also had to make all the arrangements for the funeral and wake by herself since we were still en-route from New York and New Jersey. She managed to maintain her composure through the whole ordeal, and created a touching tribute along with a written program for the wake.

The program included some of Dave's writings and some family sentiments. We will always be proud of how she took the reins and handled this tragic situation. Back home, I longed to hear David's voice and suddenly recalled David had left one of his audio sermons in my home during his brief stay with us. Hence began a frantic search to find this tape.

Looking down at the tape for the first time, I realized the title of the message was "True Biblical Waiting." Never having heard the message, I listened for the first time anxiously awaiting the sound of his voice, and as he spoke I could not believe the message and that God was using David's very voice to comfort his family and assure us that David was with his Savior, Jesus.

The sermon spoke of Job, a man of God acquainted with pain and much suffering. A man that despite losing everything, his children, health and his wealth, would not curse (accuse) God and accepted not only the good, but the bad that God allowed. Job confessed, "The Lord gave and the Lord has taken away, blessed be the Name of Lord."

After David's death we listened to David's other sermons and even played various ones at his wake. It was an opportunity for David's family and friends to hear God's Word directly from David's mouth and we prayed lives would be changed in the hearing. During the last day of the wake, the Pastor gave a salvation call and many who attended surrendered and rededicated their lives to Christ. We understood that amongst a mother's cries and a father's heartache, God would use even this for His glory.

Scripture References: "By wisdom a house is built….If you falter in times of trouble how small is your strength." (Proverbs 24: 3-10

"I am the vine; you are the branches. If a man remains in me and I in him, he will bear much fruit, apart from me you can do nothing" (John 15:5.)

What Am To Do Lord?

*David's Notes: Written to open our eyes to our self-worship and
so that we could be Christ centered, not us centered*

I sit here today; I'll sit here tomorrow,

Not knowing what to do, Lord?

What could it be, what chance do I have,

Am I on the right track Lord?

Should I do something that attracts you?

Do I have to yell at you so you can hear me?

Do I have to scream at you to get your attention?

Do I have to do anything to know you Lord?

Maybe I'm just too far away,

Or maybe I'm getting close Lord.

Do you really want me to know you Lord?

Should I become stronger in you or weaker Lord?

What am I to do Lord?

Please won't you tell me Lord?

I have heard about what you did for me,

I have heard about why you did it,

I even have begun to believe it too.

But, I don't know now because,

I haven't heard from you Lord.

Just tell me Lord, please could you Lord?

Maybe I should pray less, or maybe more Lord?

I'm so concerned about myself Lord.

What am I to do Lord?

What? Did I just hear a voice?

Could it be or is it just me?

I guess I'll just let it be Lord.

What? There it is again, that voice.

Lord, why don't you tell me what to do?

Lord, I know you love me and died for me;

I'm just getting depressed about my situation,

And I'm starting to, dare I say, doubt my faith.

I do not doubt you, just my walk with you.

Is it all it could be, or am I not worthy of you?

Are you not talking because I'm not living right?

Maybe, but dare I say, after all I don't want to be called prideful,

But Lord I'm not living in sin, so why this silence?

I know you said you would give me,

Your abiding peace even in the midst of my storms.

And I thank you for it, Lord.

And I also know you said in your word,

Your grace is sufficient for me.

But Lord, tell me what do.

What, again with that voice?

Lord what am I, Samuel?

Could it be you're trying to tell me something Lord?

"Here I am," tell me.

Lord I'm listening, don't give me silence again.

Oh well, I tried Lord, but you didn't tell me.

You told me nothing,

Except simple faith things and then silence.

Wait a minute; you did speak to me,

You spoke to my heart.

I did hear your voice, but didn't want to listen.

I witnessed your silence, as well, but didn't listen.

I now know what to do Lord.

I need to put simple trust in you Lord.

I need to be silent before you,

So that I can hear your still small voice Lord.

I'm sorry Lord,

I expected the earthquake, the lightning, the thunder,

But you wanted my heart stilled before your presence,

So that I could hear your voice,

And know the grace you've given me.

I was only concerned with myself,

And allowed pride to build a wall.

I couldn't hear you,

Because I was trying to do it myself,

And you were trying to tell me,

"Apart from me you can do nothing,"

It's not in works or in doing things

That you receive acceptance,

But you already had it,

Because of my finished work on the cross.

You condemned yourself,

According to your own thinking,

Of what was right and wrong.

But my blood has given you an eternal redemption.

Therefore, there is no longer,

No condemnation for you who are in Christ.

For my Spirit has set you free,

From the law through me.

Lord I spoke and I mumbled,

I rattled and I rolled too.

I complained and was dismayed,

But now I overcame all my fears,

I know what to do now Lord?

I'm supposed to get to know you.

The loving grace and mercy shown me.

I want to know you Jesus,

So that I can know true love and peace,

So that your gentleness will give me rest,

Even from myself.

Lord, your voice is sweet,

And I humbly come to your feet.

I'll not toil or faint; I'll just rest and obey.

What am I to do Lord?

I'm to listen to you.

Not my own understanding and ways,

For your ways are not my ways.

For my way is struggle,

But your way is peace.

That's what I'm to do, Lord.

For in you there is truth and rest for the weary,

And in my own strength there is barrenness.

So Lord, I will trust in you and your ways,

And you will make my paths straight.

So what am I to do, Lord?

I am to live by your grace!

Written by David Chaluisan on 1/31/93 at12:23am
Additional Scripture References: Isaiah 55:8; Proverbs 24:3-10;
John 15:5

CHAPTER SEVEN

RENEWED

Glimpse: As a Christian, we must ask God to control our natural instinct to judge, especially our brethren. We are so judgmental that we feel the need to compare all Christians to our preconceived ideas of how a "Christian" should live, behave and look; not a position we should take. In the book of Job, after Job experiences tragedy upon tragedy, his friends accuse him of doing something to provoke God's wrath and Job feels totally abandoned by those around him. David speaks about this in his sermon, "True Biblical Waiting: Part 2."

A couple of months prior to my brother's death, I wrote a letter to Reverend David Wilkerson, a man of God my brother admired and he attended his church in Times Square for some time. In my preconceived ideas, I felt this letter required writing.

In this futile, yet genuine effort, I mentioned my brother's time of testing in leaving Queens and relocating to Florida --- never imagining that all of David's steps were precisely moving in the direction God had ordained even if it seemed like David had lost his ministry and dream. I sent David a copy of the letter, thinking I was helping get David on the so-called, "right track."

As I saw God's plan unfolding after David's death, I would later regret that letter and David and I never spoke about it. You see David's brokenness taught him to obey God and humbly submit to His mission. How many of us would have reacted with pride and retribution? How self-righteous are we to think that we could interfere in what God is doing in and through a believer's life; one walking in humble submission to his maker and in peace with his Savior? Our sovereign God is quick to rescue those who choose to Obey Him and will restore!

Scripture Reference: "O Earth, do not cover my blood, And let my cry have no resting place! Surely even now my witness is in heaven, and my evidence is on high. My friends scorn me; my eyes pour out tears to God. Oh that one might plead for a man with God, as a man pleads for his neighbor! For when a few years are finished, I shall go the way of no return."(Job 16:18-22)

Renewed Again

I sit here in my hotel room, saddened by the news.

News that has hit straight to my heart.

I'm lonely, so down and just scared,

I'm trying to forget the past.

I'm crying out to Jesus, have mercy on me.

According to your unfailing love,

Cleanse me deep within.

Renew me, Lord, way down in my soul.

So down to the fibers of my very being.

I will be made whole again.

Renew me again oh Lord,

And create in me a pure heart.

Oh Lord, Your Word says,
"The Blood has made me white as snow."
It was the perfect sacrifice.
The Blood renewed me, once for all,
Despite the way I feel.
So even if the world attacks,
Surely God will help.

Renew me, deliver me, and sustain me,
With your very hope!
For the Blood of Jesus has made me new.
I'm a righteous Son of God,
Even though I make mistakes.
He tells me deep within my soul,
"I'll remember it no more."
In me you'll find no condemnation,
For I took it all at Calvary's hill.
So just turn away and start again
You're renewed and born again.
For though men may forsake you
I never will, for I'm Jesus, your friend and hope.
I'll never leave your side, for my Spirit lives in you.

In me, you'll never hear, the words forsaken.
For I love with an unfailing love,
That you'll never fully comprehend.
So begin again, unafraid,
For my Grace has made you whole."

So I'm here to say, just rest and obey.

So I'll glorify your name, Oh Lord,

I'll glorify your name, Oh Lord.

The name that is above every other name,

Right to my dying day,

I'll forever be changed,

And then I'll be escorted into heaven,

Renewed forever!

Written by David Chaluisan, Jr. 11/11/94
Additional Scripture Reference: Deut. 6:5, Matt. 22:37, Ps. 103:3, Ps. 110:3, Ps 118:6-7, Col 3:3, Heb. 9:12, Col 3:4, Ps 45:4, Ps 42:2, 44:3, Ps 14:1

CHAPTER EIGHT

RIDING THE HEAVENLIES

Glimpse: The last summer my brother David and I spent together in Florida, I asked him to take me to the local Christian bookstore to purchase a specific cassette, "The Light Inside" by Gary Chapman. Making our rounds in the various Christian bookstores was something we all enjoyed during our Florida visits because the Christian bookstores in Long Island and the City are practically non-existent.

Upon our arrival in Florida, following David's death, I entered David's room and my eyes caught a glimpse of that same album on David's dresser. Apparently David had a copy of this album as well. A particular song on that album was called, "Sweet Glow of Mercy" and its words were so timely and compelling especially towards the end of the song, "If I should die before I wake, there is no doubt what soul He'll take, there'll be a sweet glow of mercy that covers me."

Rev. David Chaluisan went to sleep one day and never awoke here again, but in reality, Rev. David Chaluisan went to sleep here on Earth and became fully alive for the first time upon his arrival before His King and Savior! I felt this was God's way of reaffirming David's ultimate destination. Not that we required an affirmation, but our Lord knows our deepest needs at each particular nanosecond of our lives. He knows how emotions and fears overwhelm his children when tragedy strikes. He is a most compassionate God.

Scripture Reference: Deuteronomy 6:5; Matthew 22:37; Psalm 103; Psalm 110:3; Psalm 118:6-7; Colossians 3:3; Hebrew 9:12; Colossians 3:4; Psalm 45:4; Psalm 42:2, 44:3; Psalm 14:1.

Riding the Heavenlies

Our God is rising up an army

That is totally devoted to Him,

Heart, Mind, Soul and Strength.

Our God rides the heavenlies

He rides on the wings of the wind (Ps. 103:3) (Ps. 106:30)

God Makes the Clouds His chariot.

Our God wants troops that are willing to fight

in the day of battle. (Ps. 110:3)

Troops not afraid or dismayed at the enemy,

But looking with triumph on the enemy, (Ps 118:6-7)

For what could they do to me, if God is with me!

For I am a dead man to the world (Col. 3:4)

But made alive by the Blood of Christ. (Heb. 9:12)

Christ, who now, is our life

For He rescued us from our hopeless state of living.

Our very life itself is now hidden with Christ in God.

So when Christ, who is our life, appears

We will go riding the heavenlies with Him.

In His majesty He rides the heavenlies victorious.

On behalf of truth, love and grace, (Psalms. 45:4)

Our God rides forth in love for his people,

A love that will never fade away or decay.

It's not by our arm's that will bring us victory,

But it's by the right hand of the living God,

Through Jesus Christ our Lord. (Ps. 42:2; 44:3)

For the Light of Christ will shine through

The darkness of this world,

And in His glorious face,

We will be strengthened,

Because of His radiant love.

For He is our King and our God, who became like his own,

To save us from death's call.

So we give our hearts totally to You,

For You know the secrets of our hearts.

We humble our egotism and prideful way of living;

Which was to disregard God and his existence.

For the fool says there is no God. (Psalm 14:1)

But we know our God reigns evermore.

So when He returns to take us home,

It will be with the shout of the archangel,

And it will be a triumphal entry from the heavens above.

We will see Him as He rides,

The heavenlies to make us free.

We will go shouting into glory,

Hosanna in the highest.

Blessed are you Lord,

Jesus who came and delivered us.

You opened your gates of righteousness on our behalf,

And made the way for us to enter into our reward.

We enter in not because of our works or our position,

But because of Your living grace.

Given to us who believe and accepted,

Your son Jesus as Lord of Lords and King of Kings.

So we will go riding the heavenlies, with our Savior

Christ Jesus the Lord forever more.

Written by David Chaluisan, Jr. on 5/2/94 at 3:53pm

Additional Scripture Reference: Psalm 45:4; Revelation 6:2; Revelation 19:11; Deuteronomy 6:5; Matthew 22:37

CHAPTER NINE

THE GOD OF LOVE

Glimpse: David's sister Marina penned the following after David's passing:

The Sunday David passed away was Palm Sunday. I was scheduled to sing a particular song, but the tape had an issue. Instead I sang "Postrado a sus Pies" which means "I bowed on my knees," by Michael English. I would learn that evening how God had ordained for me to sing that song and its powerful significance. The lyrics I sang hours before David went home were haunting, but yet they were words of reassurance for my soul:

> *"I dreamed of a city called Glory.*
> *It was so bright and so fair.*
> *As I entered that gate, I cried holy.*
> *All the angels met me there*
> *And They carried me from mansion to mansion.*
> *And all the sights I saw*
> *I said I want to see Jesus.*
> *He's the One who died for all.*
> *I bowed on my knees and cried Holy, holy, holy...*

When I entered the gates of the city.
My Loved ones all knew me well.
They took me down the streets of heaven.
All the saints were too many to tell
I saw Abraham, Jacob and Isaac.
Talked with Mark, sat down with Timothy
But then I said, I want to see Jesus.
He's the One who died for me…
I bowed on my knees and cried Holy, holy, holy
I clapped my hands and sang Glory, glory, glory…
Glory to the Son of God."

That evening my daughter Julie answered the phone and handed it to me. My sister Becky was crying and told me something was wrong with David. As my friend drove me to my parents' home, I saw the firemen, ambulance, sheriff's office, and the coroner were all there. I walked in and saw my mom and my sister Becky crying in the living room.

The ambulance had pulled out, and I asked my mom where Papito (dad) was. She told me they had just taken him to the hospital because he had suffered a mild heart attack. It was a nightmare and I thought I would wake up and everything would be all right, but it wasn't.

I went to the hospital to see my dad, and found my pastor in the waiting room praying for him. Standing in the middle of the emergency room, I asked God to let me know that my brother was okay and to please not take my dad at the same time. Then I remembered the song I had sang in church earlier that day and was reminded that my brother was in the best possible place, in the arms of our Savior.

My brother was quiet, simple, and very bright. He was never attached to the material things this world had to offer. He accepted Christ when he was 11 years old. He took correspon-

dences in Biblical Studies without our knowledge. He also got involved with the local church and joined the youth group and various activities.

He looked up to Pastor David Benke and I guess he became an inspiration to him. He was later ordained in his early twenties at Times Square Church in New York City. Our parents were happy, and me and my other sisters were happy, but surprised being that none of us knew the Lord. Us girls had always attended church, but never knew what serving God really was. You could ask David questions about any topic and he would always have an answer for you, whether you agreed or not. He was not perfect because we had our share of arguments and disagreements, but I still looked up to my brother even though I did not show it at times. I knew he could do anything he put his mind to. He was an artist, writer, huge baseball fan, great son, wonderful brother, and pastor. He loved his nieces and nephews and loved spending time with my daughter Julie and all the children.

As I look back on our childhood and all the time David, Becky, and I spent together, I laugh and thank God for those moments. As the three youngest, we spent the most time together as my dad enjoyed taking us to Flushing Meadows Park to play ball or to the City during the Christmas season. We would take pictures with Santa and enjoy the beautiful window displays in Macy's and the Christmas tree lighting at Rockefeller Center. All the tears and laughs we shared were still no match for his passion and wisdom when sharing a conversation with David about the Lord. The love of God could not be contained in this servant of God!

--- Marina (David's sister)

The God of Love

The God of love flows from above,

To give us his love, which flows on and in us.

He is the meaning of true understanding,

He is the meaning of True agape love,

He is the meaning of our life.

He came and loved us,

He came as one of us.

So we would have true life and love.

Because He first loved us,

We in turn must love one another.

For in Him, we are one body.

This is how God showed his love,

He sent his one and only.

So now our lives are hidden in Him;

We now live life with meaning because of Him.

For Jesus Christ atoned for our sin, once for all.

If we believe that Jesus Christ is God,

God lives in us and we are set free.

Because God is love, we have no fear.

For fear fades away with true love.

We have passed from death to life,

Because of Jesus Christ and the love of God.

So we must love and continue loving,

For we know the true love that

He has lavished on to us.

So we are called children of God;

Not yet known, but purified in Him.

So the God of love will be heard through us;

By our love they will know Him well.

So live in love and speak in love to all.

For then through us, God's love will shine,

It will shine like stars to the nations.

So remove all your hang-ups, hate, bitterness and fears.

Then you will learn to love as He loved.

Your actions will move mountains of hate with the love of God.

Then the God of Love will rejoice forever more!

Written by David Chaluisan, Jr. on 1/2/93; 1/20/94 at 8:28pm

CHAPTER TEN

GUARDIAN ANGELS

Glimpse: God's hand of protection was evident throughout David's life. David frequently referenced some of the events below in his sermons and writings. These incidents served as reminders to David of God's faithfulness. We are often predisposed to dismiss events as mere coincidences or happenstance; we boldly claim that God's hand had no part in this. A well-known pastor put it best when he stated, "a coincidence is an event in which a sovereign God chooses to remain anonymous."

As for me, I am fully convinced God's sovereign hand was interceding on behalf of this future servant!

During David's childhood days, he and his younger sisters were quietly playing with their toys on the bedroom floor when he recalled seeing a strange man enter the apartment and look around. At the time, Mom was out and Dad was sleeping after exhaustively working a midnight shift.

David, being the little man of the house, threw one of his toy cars at the man and later recalled how the man turned around to look at him, then ran out of the apartment. As David entered ministry, the Lord reminded him of that incident. The Lord said, "Do you know what that man saw when he turned around?" God told him, "I have kept you since you were in your mother's womb. Do you have any idea what that man saw that caused him to flee?" David never forgot the incident and the Lord's gentle reminder.

Another time when David was 8 years old, he was running late for school and Dad decided to walk him. On the way there, Dad stopped in front of this grocery store and decided to go in. Mere seconds after stepping into the store, they heard a crash and they ran out to see what had happened. They saw a car on the sidewalk right next to the store. The neighbors said the car came barreling down the street and smacked into that spot. Normally this street had many pedestrians with most of the city children walking to school, especially since it was only about six city blocks away. However, that morning, not one person was walking on that side of the street. As a matter of fact, onlookers pointed out to them they were the last folks to walk on the spot. David was so shaken that Dad decided to take him back home, and as you could imagine, Dad was quite shaken, as well.

David loved softball and one afternoon as he and his two friends were walking back from the field, they were suddenly surrounded by two guys who thought one of David's friends resembled a person that stole his sister's necklace. The guys pulled out a sawed off shotgun and hit one of Dave's friends with the side of the gun. These two guys continued to address David's friends and never even looked in David's direction. Throughout the whole ordeal, David remained still, even though he was tempted to start swinging his bat.

When the guys realized they had a made a mistake, they let them go. David's friend later commented that the perpetrators never made any threats to David and they said it was almost as if they did not see him despite the fact he was standing right next to one of the guys. David knew the Lord then and later acknowledged God's protection.

One afternoon David was driving from Queens to Staten Island to visit our sister Cindy when he heard a pop. Not feeling any difference in the car's motion, he continued driving and even went back home safely without detecting any obvious issues. That evening, Dad took the car to work during his overnight shift. When he returned in the morning, he came over to David and asked him what happened to the tire. David was puzzled and did not understand what dad was referring to. When David and his dad went out to look at the car they could not believe what they were seeing. As they looked down where the tire should be, there was only a rim. David had continued his trip to Staten Island and back home to Queens on a rim. David was humbled once again by God's protection.

Another faithful day, David offered to drive me to the ER because my six-month-old son was running a very high temperature. My husband Danny was working in the hospital and was going to meet us at the entrance. While stopped at a red light, we felt a hard blow to the back of the car. Then the pushing started and we realized we were hit from behind and were being dragged by the other vehicle.

When our car finally came to a standstill, David appeared fine and the baby was still on my lap and my arms were wrapped around him. We appeared fine, but my 4-year-old who was in the back seat had been wedged underneath the seat and was terrified! -- but thank God he was fine. We were told the driver tried to get away, but finally stopped down the block.

As David ran out of the car to see what was going on, he nearly passed out from the blow to his head. He then spoke with the po-

lice, and mentioned to the officer that a couple of weeks prior he was driving a Volkswagen until it broke down. My father and David went on to purchase an Audi from a cousin they had not seen in years. The police told David had he been driving the smaller Volkswagen, we probably would have been killed or severely injured. Although the Audi was totaled in the accident, we walked away. David did not join us on the ambulance because he wanted to ensure he was home when the car was taken back to the house, so he could explain to Dad and tell him we were all fine. Other than some bumps and bruises we would all be unharmed. God's amazing protection once again!

Guardian Angels

Guardian angels, who are they?

Are they ancient mysteries that we know nothing about?

Are they just myths proclaimed by man,

Then through the ages progressed to something bigger than us?

Are they true angelic beings given to us,

From far up above for our protection?

What exactly are they made of, are they flesh or spirit?

Why exactly are they given to us, or are they?

Does God assign one to everyone under heaven appointed to be?

So that when we're born, we're not alone in the earth.

Do we really understand fully what angels are about?

I believe we don't have universal wisdom that transcends the ages,

But we only have our human wisdom to get us through.

But you may say there is another wisdom given to man.

Yes, you're right, God does give us another wisdom,

But it is only given to those who accept Him.

It's a spiritual wisdom given to our hearts,

So that we may know spiritual things from above.

But even that wisdom is given in part, so rest, for you're not God.

Today everyone speaks about angels.

Many claim to even see and speak to them too.

But which angels are they speaking to?

For there is more than just one type of angelic being.

They are in our world every day, even if you can't see them.

All the same, they are there, in the spirit realm.

But are they heaven's messengers or the devil's spawn?

Angels all were made the same by the creator.

In creation they were heaven's guard;

In the devil's fall from heaven, some were misled.

Some were changed and are hell's army today.

Which one are you speaking to?

For remember, even the devil masquerades as an angel of light.

If you are speaking to or seeing one, remember they may look like a lamb, but it may be a lying snake.

The devil deceives and rejoices in his game,

So be careful to test the spirits and make sure they're heavens guard not the devil's spawn.

Guardian angels just who are they?

How do I tell one from another; only by God's wisdom.

Could they be my savior's in time of trouble or my destroyers in disguise?

Heaven's guard will not be worshipped.

They will not allow us to worship them,

Because they are created beings just like us.

For when the Lord returns, we will judge the angels,

Not them to us, so keep this in your heart.

Heaven's guards are fellow servants with us,

But the devil's spawn will gladly accept praise from men.

Guardian angels are sent as messengers, and then to depart;

They will not fraternize with us, why?

Because God's spirit lives in us to teach us all truth.

For if we need more wisdom or understanding,

God's Spirit will do the teaching.

Our guardian angels will acknowledge Jesus has come in the flesh.

They will tell you He is God, and will only glorify Him.

Anything less is not blessed.

For our guardian angels will only be messengers of God's,

Wonderful grace and truth.

For God makes his angels like the wind,

And his servants like flames of fire.

For fire purifies and brings forth truth.

So you will know who are heaven's guard and the devil's spawn.

Our guardian angels watch over us, mostly unknown.

They protect without name.

We cannot understand matters about celestial beings,

For the spirit world is unseen.

Unseen for our rest and solace.

For God knows we are treasure of clay,

And in His infinite mercy He has blinded us to battles unknown.

For our hearts would melt with overwhelment,

At this sight too awesome to comprehend.

So in this world we see only in part, to save our life.

But when we cross over to the other side,

We will fully see only when this life is fully over.

Will our spirit be guided through this unseen world?

Then with our guardian angels leading the way;

Protecting us from hell's spawn,

We will reach our heavenly goal.

And as we meet our Savior Jesus,

Our guardian angel will rejoice.

For his service here on earth has been done,

And the words good and faithful servant,

Will echo through the heavens forever more.

By David Chaluisan, Jr. Title written on 8/94; Poem written 10/22/94

Additional Scripture Reference: Isaiah 14; Ezra 21; 2 Peter. 2:4; 2 Corinthians 11:14; 1 John 4; 2 Cor. 11:15; Revelation 22:8-9; Hebrews 2; Hebrews 1:7; 2 Peter 2:10-11.

CHAPTER ELEVEN

WALK THIS LAND

Glimpse: David stayed briefly with all his sisters and since he was not working at the time, he took on the role of babysitter for many of our children. He cared for my children during the day while my husband and I were working.

At the time, David was without a car and had to walk a mile or more with my youngest. David pulled the antiquated Radio Flyer wagon with Nick in it from the home to the school every single day without a complaint. As David pulled that little red wagon, my son would squeal with joy as he sat in the back. What an amazing uncle and caregiver was their Uncle David! We adults did not fully understand David's call since most of us were not walking with the Lord at the time, but if you ask any of them, they will tell you there is no doubt whose life their uncle mirrored!

After David's death we found some of David's poems in the desk of my oldest son, Dan Jr. This same room had been David's room during his stay in our home. Discovering those precious poems years after David's death, was like receiving a letter from David. During David's wake, my son Joshua David, only 12 years old at the time, memorized Psalm 91 and recited it for his uncle.

David never had children, but his legacy will continue through these young men and women: Danny Jr., Joshua David, Nicholas J., Justin Michael, Julia Marina, Domenico Rocco, Kayla Alexandria, Analisa and Brooklynn Grace. The love their uncle David had for Christ will forever be imbedded in their hearts and will be passed, similar to a baton to their children's children.

Scripture Reference: God is a covenant keeping God -- to those who serve Him. "He remembers his covenant forever, the promise he made, for a thousand generations." (Psalm 105:8)

Walk This Land

He came so humbly into our midst,

The little baby who would know him.

He came and dwelled among us,

He grew and walked this land,

This land so beautiful and lost.

As Jesus walked this land,

Many were blessed and believed as He went,

He blessed, He delivered, and He set, men's hearts free.

He became the talk of the land.

Who was this young man?

Was He just a carpenter's son or the son of a foolish young girl?

Was His claim so hard to bear, for He came at a time of need.

The night of the prophet's visions were over?

For the day had finally come, their visions and dreams were fulfilled.

It was fulfilled in the life of Jesus our King.

In the dwelling of the righteous, the prophets shouted for joy,

For their visions of hope had come.

Though no one could see them, in the world beyond, their voices echoed through the wind;

"Our Savior, our Messiah, our King has come!"

In the heavens the angels rejoiced,

As the mighty one of Israel, had appeared to walk this land.

Rejected, mistreated, and ridiculed;

Yet He walked the narrow way for us,

Because of a love that could not fade away.

Jesus suffered temptation,

So hard to explain, yet He was without sin.

He endured all things, things so ugly for this man of peace.

He begun through His suffering and grew deep within,

For the Holy Spirit caused Him to sing,

And in spite of all the pain, He knew it was Him,

For only He, could free man from their sin.

So He walked Golgotha's Road, right toward the cross.

He bled and died, but He rose and He lives!

So we believe and receive;

For when Jesus comes to our hearts

Then we can sing.

In spite of our sufferings we can now live.

We live, because He walked this land.

Written by David Chaluisan, Jr. on 7/23/94 at 3:42PM, 8/15/94 at 8:05pm

Additional Scripture Reference: Psalm 46; Psalm 14.

The March of Ruin

For every life, there is a death.

The March of Ruin has no favoritism, it knows no color.

All it knows is the remains of the soul.

What might have been, melted into the night.

For the March of Ruin seeks you tonight.

It roams the earth, out to devour anyone available for duty.

For our hearts play into the fire,

For the fire consumes every life.

It has no barriers, just the delight,

The delight to consume, has come for you tonight.

You have no fight to give just the horror of the night.

For then March of Ruin seeks you tonight.

What can you do, run from the night?

You can run, but you can't hide.

For the March envelopes you, partakes of you,

Embraces you, consumes you and forsakes you tonight.

You cannot fight what you cannot see,

For the barriers of time and dimensions shield our very eyes.

We are like sheep lead to the slaughter,

blinded like a bat in the light we live, yet cannot see.

For the eyes of the spirit are dead to you and me.

Yet one still exists that can stop the March of Ruin.

Which leader in the world could it be?

Is it the new leaders ready to arise in the world of nations?

No, for he will bring the March of Ruin to a new height,

By deceptions of light at noontime.

But his true colors soon will show toward the night that blooms.

For none of the world religious leaders of the past could stop the March of Ruin.

None of them claimed salvation's way.

None were sure of their own way,

Let alone, for the whole human race.

But, yet one still exists.

Oh, who could it be?

Written by David Chaluisan, Jr. 11/11/95 at 11:09am and 4:35pm

By Just the Power of His Word

Words are far more powerful than we can ever perceive. (Proverbs 13:3)

For by words, many were put to death, sentenced to die by the power of a word.

Emperors, kings, and queens had power to kill, with just a word.

For their loyal subjects would gladly carry out their command without hesitation, but by just the power of a word you could also have life.

For by the tongue you can spurn out death or life.

Many of us use the power of a word to bless, but also to curse.

We have all said kind words of encouragement and love at some point in our lives.

We have also used the power of a word to say mean and hateful things at other times in lives.

So we know how words affect our lives.

They can bring down, but also exalt us.

About 2000 years ago, there came a man who would change the course of human history,

And impact the universe by just the power of His words.

By just the power of His word He would give of himself with what God had freely given.

He would live among us for a short while, about 33 years; although He had always been.

Yet He came and dwelt among us to give us a new way of living that would change the way of mankind forever.

As a child the power of His words melted the hearts of men from stone to flesh.

His wisdom was beyond our understanding, yet we didn't fully understand His powerful words.

We mumbled about His ways as we grew with Him.

He grew into manhood before our eyes, yet we despised His words of life.

Even foreigners couldn't grasp His wisdom and powerful words.

He riddled us with His words, like a genius, who was just simply thinking out loud.

Many wanted to hear more from this righteous young man.

For John the Baptist said He was "the one," the one who would lead us into a new kingdom by just the power of His word.

Many were changed, demons were cast out, hopeless wanderers were given hope,

And hardened criminals were changed to loving leaders full of hope.

The fatherless were no longer without a father, and the most amazing trust came by His word.

For He said, "I am the Way, the Truth, and the Life."

He was able to back it up by bringing truth to life in showing that He was the way, by giving life to the lifeless.

For He rolled the stone away, and a dead man, four days in the grave, came rolling out alive,

He praised Him as the Son of God come to Earth as, "Jesus of Nazareth."

By Jesus' power alone did many others come to have life again?

By a word of faith, the centurion's servant was healed.

For Jesus said, by just the powers of his word, your servant is healed, go home and rejoice.

Rejoice for God has sent the promised Messiah to bring forth a kingdom of light,

Not of this world and its power, but by the creator of the heavens and his majesty.

For by just the power of His word He lived and He died,

And He also resurrected from death's sting, and made death helpless and low.

For by His powerful word He defeated Death and Hades and broke the chain of corruption.

For He was the only man ever in our world to speak only blessings into our lives.

For by His word He created the world because of a love so strong.

Yet throughout the ages we as humans have always brought down envy and death to His plan of love.

Yet, He still holds out His hands to us as a loving father would to his children, as He waits for us to respond by His word to His call.

We can all choose by a word, life, but we call also, choose death by a word. (Joshua 24)

He gives us a free choice, full of grace.

For by Grace we have His kingdom in our hearts,

For by His words we have eternal life and are born again by His .

But when we reject Him we choose an eternity away from love and peace and choose an empty, dark grave full of pain.

By His word I will choose the better way for though it may seem harder to attain, it's easy on the soul.

For by it, we have an eternal soul with an eternal redemption awaiting us, as we pass from this earthly world to the next.

So rejoice my children, for by my words I give you a peace in this life that surpasses understanding.

Even in the midst of the storms of life, you are able to stand and not fall back,

For I'm always with you, giving you My words, filled with power to your very soul.

For by just the power of My words, you will see God!

For as your years pass on this earth, look up for your true home awaits you, by just the power of My word.

Despite all the troubles and hardships that may come into your life, rest your heart, in My love for you.

For I came to give you a well of living waters,

Living waters that now flow through your blood,

To supply you Godly peace through all of life's circumstances.

For I come with words of power that are sealed with heaven's guard.

They will never spoil or fade; for I spoke it by just the power of my word,

And it is so for all of eternity for by just the power of My word you are saved.

Written by David Chaluisan, Jr. 10/30/95; 11/11/95

CHAPTER TWELVE

SHELTER FOR LITTLE JANE

Glimpse: My niece Julie composed this letter to her uncle shortly after his death to express what he meant to her. She was only 7 years old when he died, but he left a lasting impression in this young girl's life as a child that was raised by a single mom. David was one of the few positive male influences in her life along with my dad, her grandfather. When she lost her uncle it changed her life, but the indelible mark David left will always be with her and will always keep her seeking after the God of her uncle, Jesus, the Savior.

"My uncle was very special to me. I was very young when he died. I only have a glimpse of that horribly dreadful night. It was March 24, 1996 and I was only 7 years old. That night my mom and I were home and it was probably around 9:30pm when the phone rang. I ran to pick it up and Titi Becky was on the line and I said, "Hi Titi, what's wrong?" She then said, "Let me talk to your mom now, Julie,' and I said, "Okay." Then my mom got on the line and they both started crying. Mom said, "Go get dressed quickly" and I said, "Why?" And she said, "Just do what I say."

So I did as I was told. Then my mom called her friend because she was too scared and upset to drive.

When we got there we saw tons of people around including the police and paramedics. I was the one getting tissues for everyone there and for some reason though, I did not cry. I just stood there thinking he was sleeping, he's not really dead. Then my mom called her pastor and his wife and they came over right away. They took me to stay with them for a couple of days so that mom could make the funeral arrangements. That night at their house I cried, I could not hold it anymore and I knew that he really was gone.

When my mom finally picked me up, I sort of felt different. My Uncle David and I were very close and I loved him very much and I loved hanging out with him on the weekends and in the summer because school was out. I remember when he would get home from work in the mornings he would eat some chips and read the newspaper and then go to bed. I loved when he would kiss my cheek lovingly and spending time with him. The night before or the Friday before he died I remember him taking me to the fair and we had so much fun.

He was a very Godly man and he absolutely adored God. He wrote poetry and read his Bible and, of course, he was a pastor. He was also a great person and just a normal person. He loved watching football and especially baseball. I love my Uncle David and I will always love him, he was not only my uncle, but my best friend. He is and was the best uncle ever to me. He was and still is a big part of my life and he will be forever. He also taught me about God and helped me see that God is the only way. This was my uncle David!

--- Julie (David's niece)

Scripture Reference: "This is the work that God asks of you: that you believe in the One Whom He has sent (that you cleave to, trust, rely on, and have faith in His Messenger" (John 6:28-29.)

Shelter for Little Jane

As I walk down the street the faces seem like a blur.

Every morning the cycle continues.

I get up, get dressed, and travel to work.

I see many things as I move from the one place to another.

All around me bodies collide, cars honk.

For the noise is everywhere, the noise of the city.

I try not to listen, but everything harmonizes together.

So to reach my destination with no disruption I must,

As most of us have learned, to fade out the noise, and cries for help.

For who is really in need?

Who is really seeking help?

They might be up to no good.

So we become numb to those in need around us,

Because of those who may abuse our kindness.

For it's easier for us to run and hide,

Than to stay and help.

For if we love we might get hurt.

So we close our eyes and move quickly,

But many come too close, and we can't avoid them.

This one little girl kept coming back to mind.

Why was she out there, what about her education?

Oh, well, I have to go work.

As the day goes by and quitting time is near,

I ready myself to head back home,

But as I walk down the street, my mind races back to little Jane.

That little child full of potential and hope,

But for how long will it last, till the hope disappears.

If I should see her again, what could I do?

Where is her mother, her father, her family?

She shouldn't be on these dangerous streets;

Streets that swallow even the strong.

Does she have shelter or a home to go to?

I need to know, I have a little girl about her age at home,

And I know her mom would go crazy if she was missing or taken

from us.

What do you do in this helpless situation?

I think I'll just pray, but I must also put my words in action.

For that is what faith is all about,

Seeing those in need and serving in any way possible.

For as a Christian I must follow Christ's example,

For He saw our need and left heaven to serve us,

For His love is too deep for our understanding.

So we walk through this life.

We love because He loved.

We give because He gave.

He gave far more than we will ever know.

As I reach home, my little girl is waiting for me,

Running to receive her hugs from daddy.

How do you express your love,

To someone so dear and near to your heart?

How do you explain to a 7-year-old about little Jane?

That's what the little tag on her jacket said in bold letters: "Jane."

My heart aches with a deep grief

Because a nation so rich has fallen asleep.

For we forget about these innocent little ones.

Many have no place to sleep.

Yet, we condemn them with our silence.

We forget with our pride,

Because we have our own little piece of paradise.

We wail on about how if they wanted,

They too could attain a little paradise like we have.

But what about all the little Jane's who have no choice?

The ones that have no voice because of the little years.

They lived on this earthly place.

How about them?

The children who are thrown in the lion's den,

They have no choice to be in this position.

So what about shelter for the little Jane's?

For there are many in this country,

If we would all do a little part.

Would there even be little Janes in this country?

Only God knows for by His grace we have what we have.

For maybe they are there for our benefit, to show our true heart.

For we know that God is not the cause of evil,

And we know the one who is.

For He's the one who has filled us,

With lies, blaming God for the suffering when He himself is the father of it!

Yet many are afraid to even mention,

That the devil is out to destroy, hurt, and kill.

But God in his grace tells us the devil is on the losing side,

Even though it may look dim in the world.

We are His hands,

We are His light to those in need,

We are to feed the hungry and give love to the fatherless.

I pray we all heed the call.

A call to arms so to speak for all the little Jane's out there.

For may God's mercy be on us all if we don't heed the call.

For just to ignore the situation is pleading guilty to the cause.

So let's remember, we are all brothers and sisters in this life.

God's love and mercy is for all.

For those in need,

Those in the depths of despair,

Even those in the lonely streets of our cities.

For God's heart hurts when we hurt.

God tells us to have a childlike faith and love for all.

As I put my two little girls to sleep,

I remember the first time I saw little Jane.

She never left my heart.

Even to this day,

When I tell her the story of the impact she had on me,

Of when I saw her on the street,

She cries and gives me the most loving smile I have ever seen.

Yes, it's true, I did see little Jane again,

And she's now part of my family.

For I knew she needed a family.

She's my adopted daughter now.

For just as we are adopted into God's family,

So will she be to mine.

For I must remember,

We are God's hands and feet for those in need,
And His ambassadors for finding shelter for Little Jane.

Written by David Chaluisan Jr., 9/5/95, 5:58pm

CHAPTER THIRTEEN

THE GLORY OF
THE LORD SINGS

Glimpse: I will never forget that day in March. Only my mother, father and I will never forget what we walked into that day in his room. All of us were in different rooms when I heard mom yell for my dad. I will never forget the sound in her voice when she yelled for dad. It made me go running to his room which was right across from my room. My dad was yelling in Spanish, "Bendito, Bendito" which is a way of saying you feel sorry for him. I just froze and then I started to shake him to wake up. By the time mom got the phone to call 911, I was in a state of shock and could not move or talk. My shock soon wore off when I saw that Dad was not looking good by the time the police and EMS arrived. I wanted to run into my dad's strong arms, but he started getting chest pains and they knew they had to take him to the hospital.

When they took him I felt so torn that I could not go with him. I could not leave Mom alone plus the police officers were asking me questions. It was not a good feeling knowing my poor dad was alone with strangers at this time. It's like I had to choose but that's when I remembered to call Mari, my sister. When she answered, all I remember saying is, "David, he's dead." I don't how long it was before she arrived at the hospital or how long it was before we went to the hospital to see dad. It seemed as I was floating in the air and was not really present. All that ran through my mind was, "Lord let this be a dream and please don't take my Dad too. Don't take both men from life!"

When we got back home from the hospital, I kept expecting David to walk through the door and tell us it was big mistake and "I'm alive." Boy did I find that was just my mind. The rest of the night and days are like a blur to me. I remember being in the bathroom and was in there a long time crying and my dad was getting worried and had cousin Denise go into the bathroom to check on me. I felt so bad for my sister Mari as well. I went with her to make the funeral arrangements for David and when I got to the funeral home and we were going to pick out the casket, I broke down and just fell to the floor crying and told her I could not do it so she had continue with the arrangements by herself. I just couldn't go inside and I felt like I was having a nervous breakdown right there on the floor, so Mari took charge of the situation since my other sisters were still on their way from New York to us in Florida. I am so glad Mari was able to stay strong and do this for us.

The weeks and months after he passed were really hard after all the family went back home. I remember seeing my dad fall apart little by little. I would walk into the living room and just see him sitting there alone just crying and my mom trying to be strong. But I know inside she was not doing well. I began to lose my appetite and became alarmingly thin. I could not concentrate at work. One day I broke down at work and could not stop crying and that began a cycle of many meltdowns that ended with me in the Emergency room, forcing me to take time off from work to heal.

Losing my brother David, my best friend, was really hard on us. I strongly believe that my dad had a broken heart over losing his only son and friend, shortly after. That is when his health started to deteriorate. He really wanted to be with his son in heaven; he didn't want to be here anymore, I saw that with my own eyes. That is why his heart was weak. I never wanted to feel this pain again, but I did the day I lost my daddy too. I know what my dad went through with a broken heart.

I never felt that pain in my chest like I did that night in July of 2005, when I lost my dad. I have felt the pain and helplessness of death and it took a toll on me. There were moments when I didn't think I could take this life anymore, but I remember what my beloved brother did for me. I remember how he fought for me to have what he had in his Jesus, and that's when my Jesus wrapped His arms around me and gave me the hope and strength to carry on here and take care of my mom until it's my time to be with Him. He gives me joy for the morning and peace in mourning. I don't know how I could do this without Jesus. That is what my brother did for me!

I will never forget the day I bought a TV unit when we lived in Florida. I had to assemble it and it was a lot of work, and I knew it would take me forever to set up. I decided to just leave the box in the garage and worry about it the next day and went to sleep. The next day when I awoke the unit was set up and waiting by my door. My brother set it up for me without telling and wanted to surprise me. I gave him such a big hug. He spoiled me and I loved it. To this day I still have my TV unit and it is special and I will have that unit with me forever! There are so many special moments, but this one is my favorite.

My brother David was such a good brother; he was the only brother amongst so many sisters. I don't know how he and Dad did it, but I think David enjoyed it, it made him feel special. In my eyes now, he was special. From a young age God chose him, and I believe that his purpose in this life was so his family could see Jesus through him. He taught me so much about the Bible and the meaning of the word grace and faith in the Christian life. He was the person I would go to with questions about God and he knew right away what Bible verse to tell me to look up; he was my Bible answer man. Before I became a Christian he sent me by mail these Bible study sheets. He would give me the sheets to do and I did them to make him happy. Then he would take me to the Christian store with him because he knew I loved to read. He would tell me to pick up any book I wanted and he would buy it for me.

Then when we got in the car he would always make sure he would play his cassettes of Christian music so I could hear it. I would get mad because I wanted to hear my dance music not his "Holy music", as I referred to it. Since he always sat in the front seat with Dad, he got to chose the music. Thinking about it now, I am glad it was that way. I didn't like it but the words to the songs were working on my brain and I even started asking to borrow one of the tapes of a Christian singer name Amy Grant.

The other artist he would put for me was Carman and I don't know how, but he managed to get me to go a Carman concert with him. It was awesome, and then his next step was watching movies about the end of the world. But even through all that, I still was not ready to give my life over to his Jesus. I kept saying, "Not now Lord, I will when I am older." My point to this is that he never gave up on me. He was doing what Jesus calls us to do; tell others about him, and not keep him a secret and be ashamed of the Gospel.

When we moved to Ocala, Florida and he stayed here in New York, I was so lonely I missed the family so much. I didn't have any friends yet and I really got into a depression. I didn't want to eat or do anything, and when I spoke to him on the phone, he heard it in my voice and knew I was sad and missing New York.

One day I received a package he sent me with five cassettes of Amy Grant, Michael W. Smith, DC Talk, and other Christian music on it. I started listening to them, started feeling better and started to watch Christian music videos on TV. He told me to start reading the Bible and to watch a program called the 700 Club on TV. I listened to my brother and it worked.

I finally said, "No more fighting you Lord, I am not going to wait, I will give my heart to you." When I did he was the first person that I called to let him know that all his efforts of not giving up on me worked. His reply when I told him on the phone was, "I knew it was going to happen, but I was wondering why it was taking you so long when you knew the truth about Jesus." Something to think about, huh? Why do we wait in light of the Truth? The Lord used my beloved brother to reach out to me and opened my eyes to see what Jesus could do in my life and and the Lord knew what I needed to combat my depression and loneliness in Florida.

So I want to thank my beloved brother for always being there for me and not giving up on me and for showing me Jesus!

He is my Hero…

---Becky (Dave's youngest sister)

The following pages are songs written by David in worship to his great Love, the Lord.

THE GLORY OF THE LORD

THE GLORY OF THE LORD SHALL REIGN
ON THE EARTH AND IT WILL NEVER FADE AWAY.
FOR IT WILL SHINE UPON OUR HEARTS
AND MOVE FROM PLACE TO PLACE

AND IT WILL GIVE FORTH LIGHT AND THE LOVE OF GOD
SO THE GLORY OF THE LORD WILL GIVE EVERY HEART.
HOPE AND STRENGTH AND RENEWAL IN ZION.

CHORUS

THE GLORY OF THE LORD WILL BE HEARD
AROUND THE WORLD
IT WILL BURST FORTH WITH POWER SO MIGHTY
THAT IT WILL BREAK AND DEMOLISH STRONGHOLDS,
AND SET MANY HEARTS FREE
SO MANY WILL GLORY IN THE KING OF KINGS
AND THE GLORY OF THE LORD SHALL REIGN

OUR MIGHTY EXPLOITS SHALL REIGN IN THE LAND
TO BE SEEN THROUGHOUT THE EARTH
JESUS CHRIST THE ONLY SON
WILL CONSUME US WITH THE JOY OF THE LORD
SO WE WILL SHOW FORTH HIS LIGHT TO THE LOST
AND MANY WILL COME TO THE GLORIOUS TRUTH
OF JESUS CHRIST OUR LORD

REPEAT CHORUS

SO COME AND RECEIVE THE GLORIOUS ONE
WHO CAME AND DIED FOR YOU
FOR IF YOU BELIEVE, YOU WILL BE SAVED
YOU WILL BE HIS HEIR,
AND ALSO PARTAKE OF HIS BLESSINGS

THE GLORIOUS BLESSING OF THE LORD
AND IN CHRIST OUR HOPE OF GLORY,
WILL BE OUR ETERNAL PEACE
HIS BLESSING TO US IS NOT OF THINGS,
BUT OF ETERNAL LIFE.

BRIDGE (ENDING CHORUS)

SO MAY THE GLORY OF THE LORD BE HEARD
AROUND THE WORLD
BURSTING FORTH WITH POWER LIKE A RIVER
TO DEMOLISH STRONGHOLDS OVER OUR WORLD
TO SET MANY HEARTS TO FREEEDOM IN CHRIST
TO GLORY IN THE KING OF KINGS
AND SO MAY THE GLORY OF THE LORD REIGN FOREVER,
AND EVER AND EVER MORE.

Written by David Chaluisan, Jr. on 1/1/94 (2:31pm), 1/2/94 (8:06pm) Completed on 2/21/94 (5:18pm)

TREASURE OF GOD
(2 COR. 4)

THE GLORY STREAMED FROM THE HEAVENLIES
IT CAME IN A FORM OF A CHILD
THE CHILD BECAME THE LIGHT OF THE WORLD
SO THAT ALL COULD BE SAVED THROUGH HIM
THAT CHILD GAVE US LIGHT FOR OUR SOULS
HE IS THE LIGHT OF THE GOSPEL AND THE GLORY AND IM-
AGE OF GOD

CHORUS

WE BECAME TREASURES OF GOD
SO THAT HE COULD BE MANIFESTED IN US
TO SHOW US THAT EVERY GOOD GIFT IS FROM GOD
WE ARE TREASURES IN JARS OF CLAY
AND TREASURES OF GOD FOR ETERNITY

BECAUSE OF HIS LOVE WE ARE MADE NEW
FOR THE TREASURES CAME IN THE BODY OF CHRIST
WHO IS THE RADIANCE OF GOD'S GLORY
SO WE NOW ARE TREASURES FOR HIM
WE MANIFEST HIS GLORY FROM OUR INNER MAN
BECAUSE OF HIS LOVE AND SACRIFICE FOR US
SO GOD HAS SHINED IN OUR HEARTS HIS SPIRIT
TO MAKE US HIS EARTHLY TREASURES

REPEAT CHORUS

WE ARE GODLY TREASURES THAT WILL WALK IN FAITH
TO PROCLAIM THE WONDERFUL GIFT THAT GOD HAS
GIVEN
GIFTS OF LOVE AND PEACE AND THE GIFT OF LIFE
THAT WILL BE WITH US FOREVER*
FOR WE HAVE GOD'S KINGDOM IN OUR HEARTS
THROUGH JESUS CHRIST OUR LORD'S SHED BLOOD
THE BLOOD THAT HAS GIVEN US AN ETERNAL BOND**

BRIDGE (ENDING CHORUS)

THAT IS WHY WE ARE TREASURES OF GOD
GOD HAS GIVEN US HIS GRACE AND LOVE
THEY ARE GIFTS GIVEN TO US FOR ETERNITY
FOR OUR TREASURE FROM GOD COMES FROM ABOVE
HIS NAME IS JESUS OUR SAVIOR AND KING
HE DIED ON THE CROSS AND ROSE AGAIN FOR US
THAT'S WHY WE'RE TREASURES, TREASURES OF LOVE
AND TREASURES OF GOD

Written 1/9/94 at 11:55pm, 1/7/94 (1:11am);
completed on 2/21/94 (4:50pm) and 6/21/94.

Scripture Reference: Hebrews 9:27

SHOUT FOR JOY

CHORUS

SHOUT FOR JOY, SHOUT FOR JOY
FOR WHAT THE LORD HAS DONE FOR YOU
FOR HE IS BEFORE ALL THINGS AND IN HIM
ALL THINGS HOLD TOGETHER
SO SHOUT FOR JOY, SHOUT FOR JOY

HE CAME DOWN FROM THE HEAVENLIES
TO GIVE US TRUTH AND LIFE
HE SACRIFICED HIS VERY LIFE
TO GIVE US PEACE BY HIS SHED BLOOD
BY THAT BLOOD, SO PURE AND HOLY
HE HAS RECONCILED US TO HIMSELF

SO NOW WE ARE ACCOUNTED

AS HOLY IN HIS SIGHT, WITHOUT BLEMISH

SO NOW WE'RE FREE BY HIS WONDERFUL GRACE

CHORUS

SHOUT FOR JOY, SHOUT FOR JOY

FOR WHAT THE LORD HAS DONE FOR YOU

FOR HE IS BEFORE ALL THINGS AND IN HIM

ALL THINGS HOLD TOGETHER

SO SHOUT FOR JOY, SHOUT FOR JOY

FOR IN CHRIST, THE FULLNESS OF GOD,

LIVES IN BODILY FORM

HE FORGAVE US, ALL OUR SINS,

WHICH STOOD AGAINST OUR LIFE

SO HE TOOK IT ALL AWAY,

ONCE AND FOR ALL AT THE CROSS

SO WE ARE NOW GOD'S HOLY CHILDREN

SO ENCOURAGE ONE ANOTHER,

WITH THESE WORDS OF GRACE AND POWER

NOW WE HAVE THE VICTORY,

THE BLOOD OF LOVE

REPEAT CHORUS (2 TIM. 1:8-11; ROM. 8:1)

BY THE POWER OF GOD,

WE ARE SAVED AND CALLED HOLY

NOT BECAUSE OF OUR WAYS

BUT BECAUSE OF JESUS' GRACE

THE GRACE THAT WAS GIVEN IN THE SON,

BEFORE THE WORLD HAD BEGUN

THEREFORE NOW, THERE IS NO CONDEMNATION

FOR ALL OF US WHO ARE IN CHRIST

SO LET US SHOUT IT FROM THE ROOFTOPS

AND MAKE A JOYFUL NOISE TO

THE LORD

LET'S JUST SAY, THAT JESUS OUR REDEEMER LIVES.

ENDING CHORUS

SO LET'S SHOUT FOR JOY

SO LET'S SHOUT FOR PEACE

SO LET'S SHOUT FOR HEALING

SO LET'S SHOUT FOR VICTORY

AND GO OUT REJOICING,

SHOUT FOR JOY

Written by David Chaluisan, Jr. on New Year's Eve 12/31/93 at 8:18pm

Scripture Reference: Colossians 1:15-23, Colossians 2:9-15

OUR CHRISTMAS TREASURE
(OUR PEARL OF GREAT PRICE)

CHORUS

OUR TREASURE IS ALWAYS IN OUR HEART

HE CAME AS A CHILD IN THE NIGHT

QUIETLY, HUMBLY INTO OUR LIVES, TO GIVE US LIFE

OUR TREASURE, OUR PEARL OF GREAT PRICE, JESUS CHRIST
(Luke 2:8-20)

WE DIDN'T PERCEIVE HIM OR RECEIVE HIM
BUT WHEN SHEPHERDS HEARD A VOICE IN THE HEAVENS
THEY ANNOUNCED HIM AND WORSHIPPED HIM
WHEN SHOUTS OF ANGELS SANG OUT
GLORY TO GOD IN THE HIGHEST
PEACE ON EARTH, GOOD WILL TO MEN
THEY KNEW HE WOULD BE OUR SAVIOUR, OUR KING*

REPEAT CHORUS

THROUGH THE AGES, MANY HAVE COME TO TREASURE HIM
BUT MANY HAVE ALSO DESPISED HIM
THE LITTLE BABY WHO CAME TO GIVE US HOPE
THE LITTLE BABY WHO GAVE US ETERNAL LIFE
HE IS CALLED SAVIOR, REDEEMER, OUR PRINCE OF PEACE
WHO HAS GIVEN US TREASURES IN THE HEAVENLY REALMS
SO IN OUR HEARTS WE HAVE OUR PEARL OF GREAT PRICE

REPEAT CHORUS

SO OUR SOUL PRAISES THE LORD, FOR OUR CHRISTMAS
TREASURE HAS COME
SO AS WE CELEBRATE THE SEASON, LET'S REMEMBER THE
REASON WHY WE CELEBRATE
WE CELEBRATE OUR SAVIOR, OUR KING, OUR LIFE
JESUS OUR PEARL OF GREAT PRICE

WE REMEMBER HE, WHO HAS SET US FREE, BECAUSE OF HIS LIFE

SO WE REFJOICE IN HIM, FOR OUR CHRISTMAS TREASURE HAS COME

SO WE COME HUMBLY TO HIM, TO ASK FOR PEACE

THE PEACE THAT SURPASSES OUR KNOWLEDGE

FOR IN OUR CHRISTMAS TREASURE, HE CAME AS A CHILD.

WE FIND ALL THE BLESSING OF LIFE, WE FIND OUR GREAT PEARL OF LIFE

Written 12/1/93 at 2:30pm in my father's car, also on 1/3/94 finished
Scripture Reference: Luke 2:28-30.

MIGHTY WARRIOR

IN HEAVEN A TREMENDOUS CELEBRATION IS TAKING PLACE THIS DAY.

ON THE EARTH NATURE IS SINGING FORTH WITH JOY

BECAUSE THE SAVIOUR OF THE WHOLE UNIVERSE HAS RISEN FROM THE DEAD

AND IS ALIVE FOREVER MORE

CHORUS

2X THE MIGHTY WARRIOR, HE HAS RISEN

2X THE MIGHTY WARRIOR IS DRESSED FOR BATTLE

2X THE MIGHTY WARRIOR IS PREPARING US, FOR THE BATTLE THAT IS TO COME

1X IT'S A WAR FOR LIFE, AND A WAR OF LOVE

THE ARMY OF GOD IS AWAKING, AND BEGINNING TO RISE UP,
FOR THEY ARE MIGHTY WARRIORS IN CHRIST
WHO ARE BEGINNING TO FIGHT
WE FIGHT WITH WEAPONS FULL OF MIGHT, GIVEN TO US
FROM UP ABOVE
HOLY WARRIORS THROUGH THE BLESSINGS OF THE CROSS

REPEAT CHORUS

THE MIGHTY WARRIOR HE IS GOD, JESUS CHRIST THE ONLY
ONE
HE CAME TO US BECAUSE OF LOVE, HE MADE US HIS HOPE
FILLED ONES
FOR IN CHRIST WE ARE SET FREE, FROM OUR DEATH AND
MISERY
FOR IN CHRIST WE ARE SET FREE, FROM OUR DEATH AND
MISERY

REPEAT CHORUS

THE MIGHTY WARRIOR IS OUR LIGHT AND HIS NAME IS JE-
SUS CHRIST
HE GAVE US HOPE FOR THE NIGHT,
 THROUGH HIS LOVING SACRIFICE
 SO NOW WE STAND HERE JUSTIFIED THROUGH HIS BLOOD
THAT GAVE US LIFE
THE HOLY WARRIOR HAS A NAME, THE NAME THAT IS ABOVE
ALL NAMES

SO IN THAT NAME WE CARRY ON, FIGHTING EVIL WITH THE SON

SO HOLY, HOLY IS HIS NAME, THE NAME OF JESUS CHRIST, THE SON

ENDING CHORUS

2X THE MIGHTY WARRIOR HE HAS COME
2X NOW WE HAVE THE VICTORY,
IN THE ONE WHO SET US FREE

2X SO SING IT LOUD AND SING IT STRONG

1X ALWAYS REMEMBER JESUS LIVES FOR YOU

Scripture Reference: 1 Corinthians 16:13: "Be on your guard, stand firm in the faith, be men of courage, be strong."

Psalm 32:8: "I will instruct you and watch over you."

Prov. 20:18: "If you wage war, obtain guidance."

CHAPTER FOURTEEN

LETTERS TO THE NATIONS

Glimpse: The phone rang. It was my sister Mari. She cried out, "Our brother is dead! Dad had a heart attack and is on his way to the hospital." I remember exchanging some words, but in my despair, I handed the phone over to my husband Mark. I can't remember anything else, but going on my knees and crying out to God. I was in shock and disbelief. This couldn't be happening.

I found myself in that place of confusion and not understanding why and how this could be happening. That same afternoon, I had received a video in the mail from the Bible Story Collection which I had ordered for my kids; the movie was Elijah. I thought back and said, Lord, was that a sign? Elijah was sent up in a chariot of fire to be with the Lord. I questioned God and asked Him, did You just take him?

Then I was reminded of the church service I watched that evening on television. The worship team was singing "Hallelujah" and it was so powerful and so anointed that it brought me into such a deep place of worship. The power and presence of God was all over me. It was so beautiful and so heavenly.

I really believed that maybe, just maybe, that was the time David went to be with the Lord and entered into His presence. After that I felt such a sense of peace!

The month before, I visited Florida. I remember going to my parent's church with David and Kay and we met my parents there. John Sterns was at the door and I didn't know him, but my brother said, hello and he greeted us with a smile and walked away to pray before his performance, or better said, before he ministered to us.

The praise and worship was amazing, I was so blessed by it. All I remember is looking over to my side and watching my brother, who was in such a deep place of worship and in God's presence. That look of love, such love for the Lord, that same look was on his face when we went to see Carman in concert in Long Island.

We had gotten there at 1pm to wait on line and to ensure good seats. The concert started at 7 pm, and when we walked in to the auditorium we realized we had front row seats! Yes, we were so excited and it was his absolute best concert. David was so blessed and so was I. That's when I saw the side of my brother that I had never seen before; he was so in his element. He was born to worship and live for the Lord.

At church that day in Florida, the Sterns concert ended and we all went up and shook hands with him. My dad shared a few words with him and told him he was just watching him on a video. David told him he was blessed and was thankful. On our way home we stopped off at Publix and picked up a birthday cake for Mom. We wanted to celebrate her birthday before I left to go back home to New York. David, Becky, and I had gone shopping together to buy mom a sewing machine. Mom loves to sew, she was a seamstress in her early days. I remember how excited

David was that afternoon about giving her the sewing machine because he knew she would love it.
To God be the glory!

"For we do not..." Thessalonians 4:13-18

I penned the words below and read them at my brother's funeral. It conveys my heartfelt sentiments:

"Thank you for bringing me to the Lord. I now have a life that is changed. Thank you for leaving your blessings in our home during those precious years you stayed with my family. Those days will always be special. My children loved you and still love you so much. You will always be part of their lives.

You had such a love for my children and your nieces and nephews! You all had such great times together. You were so special to them and their number one and that will never change. The seeds have been planted in their hearts and as they grow, a part of you will also grow in them. I will never ever stop thanking the Lord for you and my children will never forget you. The legacy you left behind will soon be known throughout the land. The Lord gave us a beautiful gift when he gave us you. I wish I had one more moment to tell you how proud of you I am, but I know that I will be able to tell you myself when I see you in heaven. I want to follow in your footsteps and I pray the Lord will give me at least half the wisdom He gave you.

So, brother, I just want to say I love you and thinking back about a month ago, I did give you a big hug and said, goodbye, I love you and God Bless you! He has you and you're at peace with Him now and even though I hurt, I will rejoice for you. I could see you up there smiling and preparing a great big church and one day we will all hear you preaching. I can't wait!"

--- Cindy (Dave's sister)

The following are letters David penned to other nations. We are not sure if they found their way to the intended destinations, but we pray they will someday.

Letters to the Nations: From America with Love, to our Christian Brothers and Sisters around the World

INTRODUCTION TO LETTERS TO THE NATIONS
2/3/94

As I write the introduction of this book of letters to my brothers and sisters in the Lord of the Nations, I'm heading back to New York from Florida on Amtrak. I'm writing this introduction, but I have already finished all the letters that God has put in my heart to write. There might be more added as God enables me. Just because your nation or city isn't mentioned, I haven't forgotten to write you. You are all in my prayers and I do have a long list of many nations and as the Lord Jesus Christ leads me and inspires me I'll keep writing to the other nations that aren't in this book of letters.

I have written these letters out of love and concern for all my brothers and sisters in the Lord of all nations. I have heard of all the sufferings and hardship that many of you as believers in these countries are going through for the cause of Christ Jesus our Lord. Our Lord Jesus Christ wants you to know in the midst of your troubles that he has heard your cries and is concerned about all your troubles. Even though it may seem like nothing is happening and your troubles seem like a mountain falling on you, know that God is a God of the valleys, but also a God of the mountains, and he can shake and move mountains, so you can go through in His name. In you, it's immoveable, but speak it in the name of Jesus; He can move mountains just by his voice. So don't become dismayed becauseit's not in your timing the way you would want it, because God has the problems in your nation, your city, your life has not faded. All is under His control and

He'll move the mountain at just the right time for your good and His glory.

Look up, for even though it's Friday, Sunday is on the way, for our Savior comes, quietly, so look up for our redemption draweth near. God bless you and keep you in his care.

I would like to share with you some scriptures that the Lord has given me during the tough times in my life, which have helped and encouraged me to go on and walk the good fight of faith. I pray they will do the same for you: Psalm 115:1, 11, 13 – 18; Psalms: 116; Psalms: 133:1; Romans 15:1-7, 13.

Your brother, David.

AFRICA
Written 1/20/94

Dear Brothers and Sisters in the Lord in Africa.

From your Brother in the Lord, in America:

May the God whom we serve in Christ Jesus be with you and give you comfort in all your troubles and sufferings for the cause of Christ.

I know it may seem like your walking in the valley of the shadow of death in your cities, but the Lord Jesus Christ has placed it in my heart to write to you by the prompting of the Holy Spirit. It may seem strange to you that a young minister of the Gospel from America is writing to give you encouragement and support through prayer and this letter of love.

I have heard of your hardships and all of the tribal warfare that has brought destruction upon your land and has left many of your children orphans. I have heard about the destruction that the plague of AIDS has had on your country and the fear that has gripped your hearts. Praise be to God who is the authority over all creation, and has not left you defenseless, but has given you mighty weapons to demolish strongholds over your country. The same God who comforts me despite my country's troubles with AIDS, as well.

God has given me comfort, so in turn I may also give comfort out to others. To you, my brothers and sisters of Africa, I give to you the overflowing in Christ Jesus. I know I may not understand what great pressure you're going through as believers of Christ in your land, and it may even seem far beyond your ability to endure. You may even want to give up the good fight of faith, but take heart, for we serve a God who has suffered for us in every way so that He in turn could uphold you in your times of trouble.

Our God is faithful and will provide you with strength and hope to overcome all of the enemy's attacks. Be on your guard, stand firm in your faith because I will uphold you through all your troubles. Continue being people of courage. Continue being strong in your faith in the midst of the storms because your cries have been heard even here in America. I want you to know that you have given me hope and renewed strength because of your obedience to Christ in the midst of the evil swirling around you.

I write to you today out of great concern and love for you, my family in Christ in Africa, I want to reaffirm my love for you and that I am praying for you so that Christ Jesus our Savior may give you victory over all the strongholds that are battling against you. I pray that God will open the heavens to you and that he will lead you in triumphant procession in Christ over all the enemy's attacks. May the fragrance of life which is Christ Jesus our Lord, be with you, to be ministers of God's grace and truth to those around you. True conversion is obedient to God's word and I pray that God will give you supernatural strength to fulfill His purpose in you.

Jesus Christ our Lord and Savior is going to cause His glorious voice to be heard in all the earth and it will be so powerful it will demolish strongholds over whole cities and regions which also includes our beautiful country.

Please my brothers and sisters in the Lord in Africa, continue in your faithfulness in prayer for it's not by might, nor by power, but by God's spirit that your nation will be set free from the cycle of destruction. I as an American have seen what lack of prayer has done to my country and God hasn't been able to move mightily in my country because we haven't prayed as a body to demolish strongholds over our cities.

We in America have become lax and comfortable with our freedom. God has brought to mind your country to me and how He is moving in spite of your trials and sufferings. I still believe God is once again going to entrust many in my country with power from heaven by his supernatural might to bring my nation to its knees, so we in America can see revival again. Don't be discouraged or dismayed for the Lord your God is with you, always, even until the end of time. God's grace will enable you to have power far beyond your own ability to endure.

Lord Jesus, let Your glory be seen over Africa. I pray for your body in Africa and that you, Lord Jesus will reign over this land and that you will consume her with Your heart, joy and love to impact her nation for the sake of the Gospel of Christ. I pray that your body will rest in your provision and the promise to come for His glory.

May the Power of the Holy Spirit fall upon you to minister to those who are trapped by the enemy's stronghold in witchcraft, false religions, and full of hate and in bondage to sin. Finally, brothers and sisters in Christ of Africa be of good cheer, love one another with God's love, for Christ has overcome the world for you and me so that we could be free from the sting of death and destruction. May the grace of the Lord Jesus Christ and the love of God and the fellowship of the Holy Spirit be with you always.

May the Lord Jesus Christ build you up and encourage you by this letter until we speak again. God Bless you and keep you in the fellowship of his saints.

From your brother in Christ,
David Chaluisan, Jr.

Scripture Reference: Colossians 1:24 - 2:23

ARGENTINA
Written 1/21/94; Typed 3/5/94

Dear Brothers and Sisters in the Lord in Argentina.

From your Brother in the Lord, in America:

Greetings, in the name of Jesus!

May the glory of the Lord Jesus be over your country and fill your hearts with peace and joy in God's wonderful grace. I'm writing to you because the Holy Spirit has prompted me to write to you, the body of Christ in Argentina. I want you, my brothers and sisters in Christ to continue in your walk of faith, for it is divine power given to us as we trust and obey to demolish all of the strongholds over your cities.

I hope that this letter will encourage you, my brothers and sisters in Argentina, for we in America haven't forgotten you and you remain in our prayers. Many of you may be suffering for the cause of Christ or even weakened in your physical bodies because of illness or attacks from the enemy, but praise God for Jesus was crucified in weakness. He lives by God's power, praise His Holy name!

Likewise, you may be weak in your bodies, yet by God's mighty power which breaks all strongholds, you will live and serve Him with might by the Holy Spirit that lives in you. Be not dismayed, for God will give you the city, but only if He is glorified and not we ourselves. I pray for you and love you in the Lord, for God's Holy Spirit has told me to pray for you (the body of Christ in Argentina).

I have heard of the spirit of witchcraft and of macumba that flows in the atmosphere of your country, and my prayer is for God to flow in the atmosphere. I pray that God's supernatural power will rest in your hearts, so that you will fight the forces of darkness over your city. For though we live in the world, we do not wage war as the world does. For our weapons are not of the world, but from the throne room of heaven itself, for we as the body of Christ have divine power to demolish the strongman and his minions and send them to flight in the mighty name of Jesus!

Please, my brothers and sisters do not let the enemy destroy your joy for we have crossed over from death to life. Praise the name of Jesus, for we are victorious warriors full of His might.

I will continue to pray for you that His precious blood will cover you and your services, meetings, and everywhere you preach the Gospel. Christ Jesus has given us an eternal covering at the cross, once for all through His blood. For the Lamb of God was slain then revealed by God to us as Jesus Christ our Savior. In these last days we in the body of Christ are a chosen generation which will see the coming of our redeemer, Jesus, our King of Kings. So praise God for giving us a living hope, for in His great mercy He has given us new birth into a living hope. Through the blood of the Lamb we have an inheritance that can never perish, spoil or fade. It's kept in heaven for us because of your faith. In the midst of storms you are shielded by God's power until the coming of the salvation that is ready to be revealed in the last days. So rejoice and be encouraged in God's promises, for even if you suffer now in the body, you will receive glory when Christ Jesus our

Lord returns for you. You have been born again by the spirit of the living, almighty God of the entire universe, you have eternity in your hearts, and you have been set free with an imperishable seed from the living enduring word of almighty God.

Continue praying, don't give up, but press in because prayer will break the strongholds of demonic powers in your cities. Jesus Christ our Lord saw the need to pray before He did anything and when the circumstances came to confront Him and defeat Him, He was ready for whatever came because he had been in touch with the Father through prayer. Jesus gave us the perfect example of prayer and obedience to the Father, so must we as a body pray, as we never have before, for the entire world.

We must pray for our leaders and for our brothers all over the world. I pray for your cities in Argentina that God will watch over your pastors and leaders in their ministry, also for all the believers in your cities as you proclaim the Gospel of our Savior. Remember you are His hands, His feet, and His voice to a dying world. Please pray for my country as well, as God is beginning to bring forth revival in our hearts again. Pray that He will again entrust America with His power to break the yoke over our cities in America. Pray for me as well in my service to the Lord.

Be open to whoever God uses to proclaim His name. Come together to pray so that you can demolish the spirits of the air in your cities. Seek the Lord above all else and declare war on the devil's kingdom and His hold will be broken and He will flee in Jesus mighty name.

My brothers and sisters in Argentina, you have inspired me here in America to sacrifice everything that I have or am for the cause of Christ, thank you for the good reports, I heard about your faith in Christ. May the God of grace who called you to His eternal glory in Christ make you strong in your faith and give you strength for the good fight of faith.

I pray for you as I close this letter which Christ Jesus has given me to give to you, out of love and concern for you. I pray that Christ Jesus continues to give you boldness and power for the sake of the Gospel in your cities.

Lord, make a way and destroy the works of the devil over this country and set the captives free by the power of the Holy Spirit. Give your body in Argentina knowledge, perseverance, and love and let these same fruits impact society in Argentina for you Lord Jesus.

May Christ Jesus' name reign over your cities and country, in the mighty name of Jesus, Amen! From your brother in Christ, David Chaluisan, Jr.

Scripture Reference: 2 Corinthians 10:3-8; 13:4; 1 Peter 1:2 -7, 19-20, 23

CHINA
Written 1/21/94; Typed on 3/5/94

Dear brothers and sisters in the Lord in China;

From your brother in the Lord in America:

Greetings in the name of our Lord and Savior Jesus Christ and may God's grace and peace be with you. I am writing to you from America because I have heard about your faithfulness for the Gospel of Christ. The Holy Spirit has given me a word for you my brothers and sisters in Christ in China to encourage you in your fight for your country. It may seem strange that I am writing to you for I have never been to your country, but the love of Christ bonds us together as brothers and sisters in Him. The Lord Jesus Christ has given me a love for you, my family in China. I have heard of all your sufferings for the sake of the Gospel of Christ and all the pain and imprisonment that have befallen you because of your stand for the Gospel of our Savior Christ Jesus. I believe God is tearing down strongholds in your country because of your faithfulness in the midst of the storms.

Your obedience to the word of God has given me renewed hope for my country America, as well. We have the word of God readily available and the freedom to preach it, but with little impact on our society. I also believe God will once again allow His power to flow in America as we yield everything to Him without fear. Please pray for me and my country that God will give us a spirit of power and remove our comfortability and give us your zeal for the Gospel of Christ.

Even though you may be receiving cruel forms of punishment and persecution for being Christians in your country, and some of you are being tortured in prisons and even martyred for the cause of Christ, still your faith and stand against the forces of evil have caused the advancement of the Gospel in your country. Because of your faithfulness for the Gospel, your women have been given by the Lord Jesus Christ, a supernatural courage and stamina to proclaim the Gospel. This may seem strange because of the laws in your country and the women's role in society, but God has chosen the foolish things of the world to confound the wise, just like He is doing with me, as I write this letter to you. The women in your body of believers has caused God to turn around what was meant for evil and to advance the Gospel of Christ Jesus our Savior.

Continue to proclaim the grace of God more fearlessly and more courageously, for the Lord thy God is with thee wherever you go. I am going to give you a prophetic word for all my family in China. It's from the Lord's own heart, given to me and probably so many others, as well to give to you: "I've heard the cries from the foundations of the world and I came to serve you, so that because of My love, you would serve Me. All through the ages I've heard the cries of My people and even in death I've made their bedsides a cathedral of faith and love for serving me. Not because they had to, but because they choose to serve Me. I'm never looking for people who have to, but for whosoever will. Make your hearts an open door to reach those who are hurt, depressed, and lost. Give my joy to them just as you have received. Put your hands around the lonely so that their broken hearts can mend because what you have received is full of life and love. That same life must spring forth from your heart, soul, mind, and strength, so that you can also give that same life to others. Hear the cries around you and serve because of the grace that you have also received. My grace is sufficient, because it's power beyond your own ability. You are to rejoice in the grace of God, not ponder it. In the name of Jesus Christ you have everything you need."

This is the word of the Lord for you and for many other countries as well. I pray this word will build you up and encourage you in all of your trials and all your service for the Lord. Know that the living God has heard your cries and He has also seen your undying faith in Him. He is with you and beside you giving you supernatural strength in all the storms you face daily.

I praise God for you my brothers and sisters in China. I praise God for underground churches that are sweeping with power from above, through your country and that is impacting your nation with the living word of almighty God even though it's difficult for you to get a copy of the Bible. You still manage faithfully to bring forth the word of almighty God to those who need to hear it.

Men of China and my brothers in the Lord Jesus continue being the spiritual leaders of your families and show those around you the hope you have in you. I continue praising God for you, for by your example God is teaching me, a young minister, 27 years old, on how we should pray as never before and also in corporate prayer in our church bodies. Just as Jesus obeyed the Father and prayed about everything, so must we as believers follow His example. When we pray, we will hear from God and we'll have His reflections in us and around us to impact society with the Gospel of Jesus Christ our Savior and Lord.

My family in China, though you are locked in mortal combat with the enemy and the powers of the air in your country don't despair for your life. For Christ Jesus has overcome the world for you to give you divine power to demolish the strongholds over your nation.

Now to Him who is able to establish you by the Gospel and the proclamation of Jesus Christ according to the revelation of the mystery hidden for ages past, but now revealed and made known through the prophetic writings by the command of the eternal God so that all nations might believe and obey Him.

To the only wise God be the Glory forever through Jesus Christ our Lord. He will keep you strong to the end, so that you will be blameless on the day of our Lord Jesus Christ, and God who has called you into fellowship with His son Jesus Christ our Lord is faithful and will never leave you or forsake you. For this reason I kneel before the Father and pray that out of his glorious riches he may strengthen you with power through His spirit in your inner being, that Christ may dwell in your heart's through faith in Him.

I pray that you may be established in love and know this love that surpasses our knowledge, and that you may be filled to the full measure of all the fullness of God. Now to Him who is able to do immeasurably more than all we ask or imagine, according to His power that is at work in us. To Him be the glory in the church and in Christ Jesus for all eternity. May God's supernatural protection and power flow through you in all of your service for Him. Even though we are away from each other, we are still one body and together we share in His promises.

Don't give up and don't lose heart for look your redemption draweth near. In the mighty name of Jesus, Amen!

Your Brother-in-Christ,
David Chaluisan Jr.

Scripture Reference: 2 Corinthians 10; Romans 8.

COLUMBIA
Written on 1/24/94

To my brothers and sisters in the Lord in Columbia from your brother in the Lord in America:

May God's grace, mercy and peace be with you in abundance, my family in the Lord, in Columbia. The Lord Jesus Christ has given me a Spirit of love for you my brothers and sisters in Christ and also for many other brothers and sisters in other countries. I know many of you my fellow brethren, minister the Gospel under great danger to your own lives and do it willingly out of love for God for what He has done for us. This continues to give me hope and courage in all of my service for the Lord Jesus Christ.

I have seen, heard, and read about all the struggles you are experiencing in your country which is the reason I'm writing to you. I want to write to the whole body of Christ in your country to encourage you so that you know many are praying for you and asking God to break the demonic strongholds over your cities and towns. I want to tell you to continue in your good fight of faith and don't allow the enemy to give you a spirit of fear or hopelessness because you are children of the living, almighty God.

I thank God for you and your faithfulness in the midst of turmoil. For many in your country are giving up their lives for the Gospel of our Savior Jesus Christ, but even though you may hear bad reports from around your country, don't give up! Look to Christ Jesus and cling to Him as never before and He will guide you through all circumstances good or bad for He is the God who will never leave us or forsake us. He is there at all times to give us a peace that surpasses all understanding. Just as the apostle Paul who wrote in Phil. 3:8, "He considered everything of the world rubbish, so He could gain Christ's eternal life."

Paul put no confidence in how things looked even if they looked really bad, but he said, in the midst of suffering, "rejoice, don't be anxious about anything, but in everything, by prayer, with thanksgiving present your request to God." Our Lord Jesus Christ gives us as His children a supernatural peace in the midst of the worst trials in our lives.

I know of the many deaths in your country as a result of the drugs in your cities. I as an American, who is also a minister of the Gospel of Christ in my country, know of how drugs are destroying my country, as well and the government doesn't even have a clue what to do about it. They don't have a clue because they refuse to acknowledge that they need God and do not pray to Him in the name of Jesus Christ our Lord to overcome all the strongholds over our country. I pray for your government as well that they will acknowledge the God who is above every creature and is the Lord of all. Please pray for me and my country as I will for you and your country. Continue to come together as believers to pray because it is only through prayer that the enemy's forces will be bound and cast out of our cities.

When we say we know the love of Christ, we must sacrifice many things just as He did for us. He sacrificed himself and left everything that was perfect and Holy for us because of His love. Christ Jesus our Lord is teaching me that, as I write to you, love is a sacrifice because when we love we aren't concerned for ourselves, but for the ones we love.

We want to do anything for them because we love them, so we sacrifice out of that love just as Jesus did for us.

My family in Christ in Colombia, if the Spirit of God lays it on your heart to pray or pray for someone, obey it for it may turn the tide of battle in the heavenlies. I love you my family in Colombia. Continue letting the love of Christ spring forth from your hearts to one another for your love has reached even to here in America.

I hope that this letter is giving you hope that you are remembered and loved by your family in Christ all over the world. In all of your struggles and sufferings for the cause of Christ, know this, that the word of God in 1 Pet. 3:14, says, "Even if you suffer for what is right, you are blessed." We are all blessed as members of God's family for Christ died for our sins once and for all to bring us to fellowship with Him and now we are called children of God, who have crossed over from death to life. All of our sufferings aren't worth comparing with the Glory that will be revealed in you and me. Even though I may not understand what you're going through and all your pains, God does and He has by the Holy Spirit allowed me to express my concerns and love for you, so that you may know God has you in mind and will never leave you or forsake you. He loves you with an eternal agape love that will never fade away, but will last forever.

You, as a believer and child of God, take a stand on who you are in Christ and walk in faith, knowing Jesus Christ our Lord has given you divine power to demolish evil strongholds over your country. As we get together in prayer to fight the enemy, for it is on our knees where battles are fought and won. So let us all, as believers in Christ Jesus our Lord, remember if God is for us who can be against us. For God has totally forgiven us and justified us by the blood of Jesus, and the sting of death was defeated at the cross and now we as believers have eternal life in Christ.

Thank you so much for hearing and reading my words of love to you. I testify that this is what God's grace is all about; loving as He loved us, no matter whom we are or where we are!

In the mighty name of our Lord Jesus Christ our King and Savior, your brother in Christ,
David Chaluisan, Jr.

INDIA
Written 1/28/94

To my brothers and sisters in the Lord in India from your brother in the Lord in America:

I send you greetings in Christ Jesus name to my faithful brothers and sisters of India and may God's spiritual blessing be with you.

I write to you today out of love and concern for you my family in Christ in India. The Lord has put in my heart, a love for all my family in Christ of all nations. He also gave me this idea to write letters to the nations so that you would be given hope and encouragement in your faith walk.

I'm a young minister in New York that is writing to you because God wants you to know that He has heard of your steadfastness and will continue to uphold you and loves you. He is your refuge in the dark days and will fulfill His purpose for you and your country. I have heard of all the hardships and persecution you received because of your commitment to the cause of the Gospel of our Savior Jesus Christ.

I want to tell you that God is watching out for you and does love you. Please don't give up, for God will go before you and will strengthen you for His glory. I know I may not understand your troubles because we in America thus far have the freedom to proclaim Christ, but I tell believers in my country not to get so comfortable because we may soon get attacked and persecuted for the Gospel. America is in a spiritual war for its life, and we need to be reminded of our faith and commitment in the midst of your hardships, so that we as American Christians will put aside our idle spirits and fight for our cities in the name of our Lord Jesus Christ, and take them for Him. Just as your country has Hinduism, Sikhs and Buddhist; my country has New Age theology, Islam and Satanism, so in a sense these teachings are ruling over our countries.

I pray right now that the Holy Spirit will open the hearts and the blinders the enemy has put around the unbelievers in your country. I pray by the power of the blood of Jesus that the demonic strongholds over your cities will be destroyed and the evil powers over your cities will be cast out and bound from your country. Continue praying as a whole body and continue in your times of intercession for your cities, for by prayer the strongholds will be broken and God will give you the city. I want to give you some scriptures that I hope will encourage you in your battles against the enemy.

Psalm 60:9, 11-12: "Who will bring me to the fortified city? Who will lead me to Edom? Give us aid against the enemy, for the help of man is worthless. With God we will gain the victory and He will trample down our enemies."

Psalm 66: 9-12: "He has preserved our lives and kept our feet from slipping. For you, Oh God, tested us, you refined us like silver. You brought us into prison and laid burdens on our backs. You let men ride over our heads, we went through fire and water, but you brought us to a place of abundance."

Psalm 68:1, 9, 19-20: "May God Arise, may His enemies be scattered, may His foes flee before him. You gave abundant showers, O God, you refreshed your weary inheritance. Praise be to the Lord, to God our Savior, who daily hears our burdens. Our God is a God who saves."

Romans 8:18, "I consider that our present sufferings are not worth comparing with the glory that will be revealed in us."
I hope this has given you hope in the midst of trouble. I pray for all the new tribal believers and the ministry of Friend of the Poor, that God will give you wisdom and provide all the needs to send the Gospel to everyone and feed your hungry. I pray for victory over all of North India and that the Hindu religious stronghold will be broken over that area in the name of Jesus. I pray also for

the young native missionaries so that the Holy Spirit will impart courage, wisdom and victory wherever they go to bring the Gospel of Christ.

Romans 15:4, "Everything that was written in the past was written to teach us, so that through endurance and the encouragement of the scriptures we (as believers in Christ) might have hope." I love you in Christ; please pray for me as I will for you my brothers and sister in India.

Romans 15:13, " May the God of hope fill you with all joy and peace as you trust in him, so that you may overflow with hope by the power of the Holy Spirit."

I pray this letter of love will encourage you in your faith.

David Chaluisan, Jr.

RUSSIA
Written 1/28/94

To my brothers and sisters in Russia from your brother in the Lord, in America:

Greetings to my fellow workers in Christ, may the grace and love of God be with you in abundance and may your hearts overflow with the joy of the Lord.

I write to you, my brothers and sisters in Christ in Russia, because of my concerns and love for you. I write to encourage you and to give you hope in the midst of your struggles.

I'm a minister from New York and write to let you know I'm praying for you and many others around the world as well. For even though we're miles apart we are one in Christ. I pray that God will daily renew your minds with His love and give you wisdom from above to continue to bring forth the Gospel of our Savior Christ Jesus to all those around you. Continue in your faithfulness to pray, for by it the iron curtain was brought down. Praise the Lord Jesus, for he has given us a living hope. I will continue to keep you in my prayers so that the 70 years of darkness in your country won't return quickly.

I'm praying that our Lord Jesus will send his angels to be with you to withhold the power of darkness trying to bring your country back into captivity. I pray our Lord Jesus will give you time and give you security to proclaim the Gospel to all in Russia, even in the New Republic and that the strongholds over all the cities will be broken in the name of Jesus!

I have heard about the Republics of Uzbekistan and Kazakhstan and the work that is being done there to bring the Gospel of Christ and to start churches to minister to the people. I pray that God gives all your workers and people divine power by the Holy Spirit to demolish the works of the devil in all the Republics. I pray that Jesus be with you and uphold, and may He give you courage and wisdom to proclaim God's grace and love. I pray also for the Uzbek city of Tashkent, that all my Korean brothers and sisters in Christ there can continue to have the freedom to proclaim the Gospel and that the Muslim government there will be set free from their blindness and come to see the true way to salvation in the person of Jesus Christ.

Father, in Jesus' name, break the strongholds over this city, Lord! Break the lying spirits' hold over the people and the government. For you my Lord are very great. For you are clothed with splendor and majesty. May the glory of the Lord flow in your land to break the works of the devil. For God's glory endures forever, and may God rejoice over your faithfulness in Him. Give thanks to God for in Him, He has given you the victory. Call on His name daily, make known among the people what He has done for you, and tell of his wonderful acts – glorify His Holy name. Look to Him for strength and seek His face always, for in Him we live and have our being. Amen!

Even here in America, God is doing a new thing. He's taking away our pride of having material things and breaking our spirit of comfortability to what's happening around us. The Lord has given me a love for all my brothers and sisters in Christ around the world including you, my Russian brethren. I write this by the inspiration of the Holy Spirit to minister hope and encouragement and let you know that God has heard your prayers and is concerned for you. Your faithfulness in the midst of your trials has filled me with hope and joy as I go through different circumstances in my life. As I write this I find myself without a job, but all other necessities of life He does provide. God is always with me and He supplies all my needs! Praise the name of our God in Christ!

I'm praying for the Nationalists in your country who want communism back ruling over your nation, and the freedom you have to proclaim the Gospel to be taken away from you. I'm praying also for the Russian Jews that they may come to know their Savior as well. I pray that the scales may be taken away from their eyes and they may see the One who is the Savior of the world. My brothers and sisters of Russia, don't lose your joy, but continue in the joy of the Lord Jesus because it will break the spirit of death in your country.

In Nehemiah 8:10 it says "Do not grieve, for the Joy of the Lord is your Strength." The Lord Jesus Christ gives us a joy unspeakable that will minister to unbelievers and bring them to life in Christ. Our joy causes the spirit of death to flee in other's lives as well as our own life. By the blood of Christ, shed on the cross, we have obtained an eternal redemption (Heb. 9:12), so Rejoice, for all over the world this Gospel is producing fruit and growing, just as it has been doing among you, since the day you heard it and understood God's Grace.

I leave you with this blessing. May God fill you with the knowledge of His will for you, through all spiritual wisdom and understanding and love one another as Christ has loved you. May the peace and Grace of God which has given us life, be with you my brothers and sisters of Russia always!

Your Brother in Christ,
David Chaluisan, Jr.

YUGOSLAVIA (CROATIA AND BOSNIA –HERZEGOVINA)
Written 1/28/94

To my brother and sisters in the Lord of Yugoslavia from your brother in the Lord in America:

I greet you with the love of Christ. I pray that the love of God overflow in your hearts and in the midst of this war. As I write to you, the Lord Jesus Christ has given me a heart of love for you and I'm deeply concerned for you my brothers and sisters of Yugoslavia. I know it's difficult to even comprehend what you're going through; all your unrest and sufferings. I want you to know that your brothers and sisters in Christ around the world are praying for you. Don't give up in this time of turmoil and conflict. I pray that God will alleviate the human suffering around you and your families. I pray that our Lord and Savior Christ Jesus will encamp his legions of angels around you and a hedge of divine protection in the midst of the slaughter that is happening around you. I will continue to uphold you my brothers and sisters in Christ of Yugoslavia.

I ask you Lord Jesus, my Comforter, in all of our sorrows and sufferings that you will comfort my brothers and sisters and let them feel your love and may they know you care for them. Give them strength, courage, a sound mind and remove any fear that is trying to overwhelm them right now in Jesus Name. Turn the enemy and his minions to flight and cast them out of this beautiful land. Remove the strongholds over this land that are causing this conflict. Father, we take authority over these demonic powers and in Jesus Name, break and tear them down and cast them out of this land and lead them to dry rugged places.

I know you are praying for your nation, but don't be dismayed, for no weapon formed against you shall prosper (Isaiah 54:17). Remind the Lord of His promises like Moses did in Numbers 14. God didn't destroy the people because he asked and reminded God about His Promises. I pray that you my God, will listen to the cry of your people in Yugoslavia.

My God I know you said in your word in Jeremiah 8:21, "That since your people are crushed, you're crushed, they mourn and you mourn." Lord, hear our prayers and their prayers and give them peace and stop the war. For you alone have the power to bring peace and melt the hearts of men.

As we're faithful in prayer, just as you tore down the Berlin Wall, you'll stop this war. We thank you in your Son Jesus Christ our Lord. Administer justice in the land, rescue the innocent from the oppressor, and watch over the children of Yugoslavia. My God don't allow evil to shed their innocent blood in the land. For you my God defend the cause of the poor, needy, and the innocent. Send your angels to them and give them charge over your little ones whom you love deeply. Be persistent in your prayers, for Jesus gives us an example in Luke 18 in the parable of the persistent widow, so we would pray and not give up. I pray for the release of hostages and that they will be returned to their families safely.

Lord Jesus, give counsel and peace to families that have lost love ones and for those that don't know where their loved ones are, uphold them in their time of trouble. Continue distribution of your word to your saints in Yugoslavia. I pray You continue

giving hope and encouragement to all in this land. I pray for the
Albanian body in Kosovo, continue working and guiding them
in their service to You. I pray for the governments' of the whole
country. Give them wisdom and love for one another so that there
may be peace in the land. Guide them to know You Lord Jesus
and to trust in Your direction, which is not for strife and war, but
love and peace.

I pray for Montenegro, Bosnia, Croatia and all cities in this land,
that God will break the chains and walls of hate, fear and death.
Break the strongholds over these cities, tear the devil's plans
down and send him to flight. Go before them, and let no arrow or
pestilence destroy your people. So don't fear for God is with you,
and will turn the darkness into light and make the rough places
smooth. He will never forsake you (Isa. 42:16: Isa. 43:1-2).

Forget the former things, don't dwell on the past. God is doing
a new thing in the land, now it springs up even though you can't
perceive it. He's making a way in the desert and streams in your
wasteland. May this word from the Lord, from your brother in
Christ in America, give you hope and joy.

May God's grace and peace flow in your hearts and be with you
always, your brother in Christ,
David Chaluisan, Jr.

CUBA
Written 1/25/94

To my brothers and sisters in the Lord of Cuba from your brother
in the Lord in America:

To my brothers and sisters in Cuba, who are called and loved of
God and kept by our Lord and Savior Jesus Christ. My love and
prayers go out to you and even though we have never met face to
face, by the bonds of Christ we are family.

I want to encourage you in all your hardships to continue praising and proclaiming the name of our Lord Jesus Christ in your country. I have heard of the economic hardships in your cities and towns. I have heard of the fuel shortages, the power failures that you experience almost daily in your country. But praise God, for I have also heard of the revival taking place in your country, the dynamic, powerful, Spirit filled body of Christ, that is rising up in these last days to minister the Gospel. I will say with you in Spanish "Aleluya! Aleluya! Gloria a Dios!"

I am also of Spanish descent, my parents were born in Puerto Rico and I was born in Brooklyn, NY and went to a Spanish Church called "La Misión," so my heart is close to your plight. I want to tell you I'm praying for you and for the Lord to continue to supply all your needs.

I know it has been more difficult ever since the collapse of the Soviet Union which supplied you with gas, wheat and other goods. But the Lord will supply all your needs in Christ because He cares for you and gave His life to show you His Love. Please my brothers and sisters continue in your fellowship with the Lord, pray as you never have before for your prayers will break the demonic strongholds over your cities. I am learning this same principle, that if I pray and my brothers and sisters in Christ in America pray, God will heal our land of all evil in our midst.

As I pray for you, please keep me in your prayers also. I will continue to pray that the spirit of "Santeria" will be broken in your country, for we have divine power in Christ when we pray to demolish strongholds over our cities. Even though things may look dim in your city because of lack of food and other goods, remember God is in control over everything and if he can feed the sparrow, he can supply all our needs. Therefore, I tell you don't worry about your life, what you will eat or drink or about your body. Isn't life more important than food and the body more important than clothes? Look at all the birds of the air, they don't sow or reap or store away in barns, and yet your heavenly Father feeds them. Are you not much more valuable than they? Who of you by worrying can add a single hour to your life? So don't worry, for your heavenly Father you need. "But seek first His Kingdom and his righteousness and all these things will be given unto you" as well. (Matt. 6:25-33).

I don't know everything that you are going through with job shortages and food shortages, etc. But as I write this, I myself have no job and no place to live, but God has continued to supply all my needs. He has allowed me to stay in my three sister's homes, as well as, visit my parents in Florida and stay there for a while. But still in my darkest hour, He has given me renewed hope and has allowed me to write this letter of love to you, for He is teaching me that when I learn to cling to Him He will be with me leading me out of all my troubles. I'm a young minister, 27-years-old who is also allowing the Lord Jesus Christ to teach me and prepare me for His purposes. Brothers and sisters in Cuba, don't give up, but continue in your walk with Christ, for the Holy Spirit has allowed me to write to you, to show you He Has not forgotten you, but is concerned for you and will supply all your needs, for He cares and loves you.

I hope this has given you hope and encouragement, for even though we may suffer for the cause of Christ here, we will all rejoice in Heaven when we meet our Lord and our Savior Jesus Christ. We will be spending an eternity with Him and experience His full love and life without pain and suffering. We have this glorious hope for the Spirit of glory lives and rests in us. Praise God!

May God's love and peace be with you for all eternity and until we meet either here or in heaven, continue in your good fight of faith.

Your brother in Christ,
David Chaluisan, Jr.

EGYPT
Written 1.26.94

To my brother and sisters in the Lord of Egypt from your brother in the Lord in America:

May the love of Christ give you faith, hope, and love in all you do. I am writing to you my brothers and sisters in Christ, of Egypt, to express my love and concern for you and all of the troubles you've experienced for the cause of Christ in your country.

The Lord has told me to write and speak freely to you, so that you would always be confident that God is for you and is always working on our behalf. I hope you will be strengthened and ministered to by this letter of love. I know of all the stumbling blocks that befall you as Christians in your country, I know that being a Christian in your country could mean even death to you.

But continue in your faithfulness to our loving Savior, who gave his life for you, so that in turn you could be reconciled to fellowship with Him as it was in the beginning of time. Be comforted in this word of the Lord "Because as Christians you're serving your country." Men will Praise GOD for your obedience which accompanies your confession of the Gospel of Christ, and for your faithfulness in sharing with them the truth that will save their souls.

Be renewed in your faith walk with the Lord Jesus Christ for He cares for you and has heard and seen your earnestness. For though things may look like they're getting worse, rejoice for we have a building from God, an eternal house in heaven, not built by human hands. So make it your goal to please him who made you a new creation. For the old has gone and the new has come through the blood of Christ, and all this is from our heavenly Father who loved you so much He gave His only son (Jesus) to reconcile us. We now have a new identity in Christ Jesus, we are children, loved and made more than conquerors and justified by his grace. Nothing will ever change this for we have an inheritance given to us by Christ Jesus that can never perish, spoil, or fade, for it's kept in heaven for you. So don't let the enemy get you depressed because of the many poverty stricken towns and the many oppressive environments that seem to grow daily.

I also want to encourage not only the adult believers, but the Lord has given me some scriptures to encourage the children in Egypt as well. To all the children, I send my love and prayers and that GOD will watch over you and send his angels to you, the little ones and that his hedge of protection will be with you.

I want to tell the children that God cares for you and loves you deeply for His kingdom is for such as you. I have heard of the conditions that many of you little ones live under and all of your sufferings. For a time is coming that you, dear little ones will no longer have to be afraid, or shamed, or humiliated. For you will be taught by the Lord and great will be your peace (Isa. 54:13). For from the lips of children and infants, God has ordained praise (strength) (Ps. 8:2). For from children comes simple faith which we as adult Christians need in our faith in Christ Jesus our Lord. (Matthew 18). See that you don't look down on one of these little ones, for I tell you that their angels in heaven always see the face of my Father in heaven (Matthew 18:10-11). May all the children of Egypt know that you are loved by many and God.

I will keep you in my prayers, God's peace and love be with you. I want to express overflowing joy in the work of many in Cairo and their work with the children of Egypt. I commend you and all of the others who are working to make the children grow up in loving, caring, supportive environments.

Remember to pray for me and my country also, as I will for you, my brothers and sisters in Christ, even here in America, which is in trouble from within. As I press on, minister, and continue preaching God's love and grace to all in His body – I hope this will give you encouragement in your lives.

In God's grace and love, peace to you brothers and sisters in Christ, from your brother in Christ,
David Chaluisan, Jr.

GREECE
Written 1/27/94

To my brothers and sisters in the Lord of Greece from your brother in the Lord in America:

May the peace of Christ Jesus be with you and give you hope, strength and encouragement in your faith. I write to you my brothers and sisters in Christ, in Greece from America to show forth my love to you, even though I'm many miles away and have never met you. I want to send you hope and encouragement in your walk with the Lord so that you will know that you are loved. All over the world, your Christian brothers and sisters are praying for you. I have heard and commend your Home Church movement which is reaching many for the cause of Christ. I pray that God will use you, my family in Christ, to reach those that are afraid to go to church buildings because of the proselytizing laws, but that they will go to house meetings. I pray the Holy Spirit will touch hearts and bring them in to hear the message of salvation and that the strongholds of religion and the strongholds of demon powers be broken from your country in the mighty Name of Jesus.

In the midst of all your trials and sufferings remember that God is in control and is fighting for you, for no weapon formed against you will prosper (Isaiah 54:17). Rejoice for if God is with you, no government, church, or leader can stand against you (Romans

8:31). When you're attacked because of your faith in Christ, count it all joy for you are blessed (1 Peter 3:14).

Even though things may look bleak around you, know that God is going to make a way out, for in our darkest hour, the dawn of light is coming to give you hope in God's promises. For God never forsakes His promises to us, but in His perfect timing He gives us a way out from the burden we may feel. May the Lord Jesus Christ make your love increase and overflow for each other and for everyone around you.

I'm a minister from New York and I'm seeing God restoring His joy and love to many in His body. I pray also that God will do that in your country and in the hearts of all those around the world who know Him as Lord. Even if the state threatens you with fines and imprisonment because of your faith in Christ and your proclamation of your faith, don't be angry or even dismayed at the state or its leadership. For Christ will make you a light and beacon to them and they will know that what you have, they need.

So be encouraged to continue in showing forth love and kindness, for your faithfulness in Christ will tear down the walls of religion and blindness of the Gospel of Christ in your country.

Be strong in the Lord and in His mighty power, continue in your prayer of faith for your land, for through prayer is where the spiritual forces of evil will be broken and bound. The forces of evil cannot stand against a body of believers united in prayer, for by the blood of Christ, our spirit has power to stand against evil spirits in Christ's name and send them to flight.Continue your service for the Lord, for your cries are being heard and will be answered for the glory of God. If God can use me to write to you from so far away and to tell you He has heard you and is fighting for you, then rejoice for you know God loves you and He careth for you.

I want to just give you a farewell greeting of love, beloved in Christ. The Lord has given you eternal life and you will never perish for no one can snatch you out of His hands (John 10:28) for you have crossed over from death to life. Rejoice in our Savior, because He comes quickly.

May God's grace and peace be with you always, your brother in Christ,
David Chaluisan, Jr.

CHAPTER FIFTEEN

<u>TEACHINGS</u>

Glimpse: As a young boy, I was very fortunate to have a cousin like David even though he was more like a brother to me. I remember always wanting to stay over his house during summer vacation, and often cried if I couldn't. We did so much together from riding bikes and playing all kinds of sports, but the number one thing that stands out was how he made sure I knew the word of Jesus. That is the number one reason, I'm so thankful David, my cousin/brother was part of life. I will never forget the impact he had in my life!

--- Raphael (David's Cousin)

The following pages contain "teachings" -- nuggets of wisdom that David wrote down. These teachings are all based in scripture and show the heart of one who desired to learn, grow, and share always the knowledge of Christ Jesus.

TEACHING ON BONDAGE

Bondage: You don't go to church because you want to get energized and stirred to get worked up, because even though you might feel great during the service, after a while when you go home those feelings and emotions will start waning. It might not be the same day, maybe it might last a couple of days, but then your emotions will bring you back to reality.

Emotions are only responders. When you leave an energy filled place they will start to come down. So you then have to go back to the service to get up again, and so on and so on. You will begin to get burned out because you will start relying on the church or the minister or choir to fill your spiritual life and your inner self.

You are then looking to things instead of the person of Jesus Christ to fill you once and for all. When you do that, you are under law. How so? Because you then are in bondage to your feelings and emotions, and you have to do something to get you closer to God. That's not grace, but law. Amen!

Written 10/23/91

TEACHING ON BRINGING THE MESSAGE
The Truth about Knowing Jesus

What is the message? What is the truth about knowing Jesus? So many people are looking for answers; hope and love, but not finding it in their lives, religion or in church leaders. Do you know why? They are looking in the wrong place. Religion isn't going to help or save them, neither will church leaders. They are there to bring the same message I'm presenting to you.

There is only one person that will save you; only one that will give you life, hope and peace in the midst of evil, and His name is Jesus! I'm talking about a personal relationship with Jesus (the One, who gave his life for us. That's right, He died for us and suffered so that we would have life.) John 3:16-18; John 10:11-18, 28-30; 11:25-26; 14:6, 27.

If you are an active church member and think by going to church you will be saved, you will be in for a real surprise. Saying you believe in God and in Jesus and the Holy Spirit as one is not going to save you. Believing is a start in knowing Jesus personally because you first have to believe in Him to accept Him, but it will not save you by just saying you believe. We have to remember that even the demons believe in God and they tremble with fear.

TEACHING ON EMPTY WORKS
DONE IN CHRIST'S NAME

All of our service has no power apart from the Lord Jesus Christ, all good gifts are from above. He's the one who imparts us with spiritual hunger and zeal to serve Him in whatever capacity because the love He has shown us.

Many of us get so caught up in our service for the Lord that often Jesus is put aside and the service becomes the all-important issue in our lives.

Serving God in the body of Christ isn't about us or the good things we do; at least it shouldn't be. I know too many who put too much emphasis on the person who's doing the serving, but that's not truth. The important truth isn't the service or the person doing the service, but the Lord Jesus being preached, manifested, and glorified to the fullest. When we serve, we must be very careful never to become so entangled in our service that we neglect to lift up Jesus, who is our glory (Colossians 1:27).

To God, the message of salvation and our service are all done in response to our salvation, to glorify His son Jesus, period! Apart from His son Jesus, it has no value because Jesus is salvation, He is sanctification, He is justification, He is life to all who receive Him (John 1:12; 1 John 5:12). God hasn't saved us for salvation or work's sake, but for the sake of His son Jesus Christ and His sacrifice and shed blood. We must deposit this in our hearts always. Everything God did was for the glory of His son, Jesus Christ, that's why apart from Christ we can do nothing of value.

Salvation and what it does in our lives isn't just something common, but it's the indwelling of God and the eternal life He has given us in His son, who is Jesus Christ. (1 John 5:11).

That's why there is no middle ground in Christianity, other religions have those middle grounds and they say there's many ways to God. The word of God tells us in 1 John 5:12, "he who has the son has life, he who doesn't have the son of God doesn't have life." Plain and simple, either you're on God's side or the devil's, you choose today who you will serve. (Joshua 24:15).

Any of our service that isn't grounded in the indwelling of Christ glorified, cannot impact God's purpose to those around us and the world. That's why Christianity isn't a doctrine or religion, but the knowledge of a person, Jesus Christ and his indwelling in our hearts, Christ in you, the hope of glory (Colossians 1:27).

TEACHING ON THE AUTHORITY GIVEN BY THE SPIRIT

Why is it that you are not walking in that Spirit; in the spirit of power and authority? I have given you a spirit of power not fear. Why are you fearing what man can do to you? Why aren't you breaking the power of the strongman in the world and why haven't you broken the power of the strongman in your lives? I'm always (Hebrews 13:5) here for you, interceding for you before my father, day and night. I'm before His throne room, waiting for your prayers to reach me, so that I can give them to the Spirit and send Him to you with power and freedom from your bondages and burdens.

Take time to know me again my children, for the night is almost over and the day is almost here when we will be reunited and be together in the heavenlies for all eternity. Many of you will lose faith if you don't spend time with me; fellowshipping with me and letting the spirit of life flow in your life through prayer. Consume My word and you will receive wisdom and courage to take you through this evil time. Rejoice and be glad because your redemption draweth nearer then when you first believed. The one who is, was and is to come.

TEACHING ON CHRIST'S REDEMPTIVE SACRIFICE

Christ died once to forgive all our sins. He shed his blood once for all our sins. He died and said "It is finished." He didn't say I'll come back every year to die and suffer all over again for you my children. No, He said it once and for all. Who, as a child of God, would want Jesus to continue to suffer? None of us would want that, that would be heartless. I can tell you it could not happen, a sacrifice can only be used once, blood spilled once. If you did that with Christ, it would be submitting him to public disgrace all over again.

All of this eliminates all hope of salvation and forgiveness, apart from a substitutionary death of somebody (which Christ did for us). With His life we have been pardoned and have eternal security because of Christ's redeeming sacrificial death on our behalf. We are set free from sin (death) and brought into life with Christ. When we do this (by his grace) not because we have done it or deserve it, but because of His grace – we then are pardoned fully 100 percent with his resurrected life. That's why we don't have to always be afraid of un-confessed sin you don't remember. Why? Because He took care of it. He said in Hebrews. 10:17, "I'll remember their sins no more."

Christ is our covering in heaven when we sin, all He does is show the father His wounds, and the sins are forgotten. (*Editor's note: This thought appears unfinished.*)

TEACHING ON THE BELIEVER'S FREEDOM

In this chapter I'll be writing about our nation's freedom and how it came about and the cost of that freedom. Then I'll focus on Jesus Christ our Lord and the freedom He spoke about.

When we speak about freedom, we must understand the forging of that freedom, why it came, where it came from, and do we have it today?

The believer's freedom or freedom in Christ is as strenuous a topic of discussion among Christians because of not understanding what the beginnings of true Biblical freedom in Christ are. Through the ages men of religion have twisted the true essence of freedom to make it mean an obligation to observe, and to grasp that freedom (Galatians 2:4-21).

We have freedom in Christ, but how far do you take it because many believers say when you mention freedom in Christ, it's allowed and it gives us a license to sin. Yes in some cases it may be abused, yes, it may be taken to the extremes. If we don't understand our freedom in Christ, it will be abused; Paul spoke about both extremes in the Bible.

In Galatians they tried to mix law with grace by human effort and abused their freedom in Christ. He gave them examples from Abraham by faith (Gal. 3). Then in Romans 6:10, he explains that we aren't to sin because of our freedom, but in 1 Corinthians 10:23 he says something that many who teach obligation to observe don't like to teach: "Everything is permissible, but not everything is beneficial and constructive."

What many have done is made a simple Gospel to confound the wise and made it a confound Gospel to the simple. You don't understand it, you're too simple minded, you need to do this and that's by our wisdom (leaders) to understand. This may be a strong statement, but let's allow the Holy Spirit to minister to our hearts about how we have grieved the Spirit of God with our revelations about grace, freedom and the law.

We have taken a pearl of great price (God's grace), and thrown the pearl to pigs. Matthew 7:6 says, if we do this they'll trample them under their feet and turn and tear us to pieces. That is exactly what we have done (Matthew 13:44-46). Thrown something beautiful away and taken in something counterfeit. We scramble to grasp what is left and turn on each other, argue, fight and tear God's grace to pieces.

Most of the time what we have left is extreme on both sides of the issue; tainted and dirty hence giving pearls to pigs.

Written 10/19/94

TEACHING ON LEGALISM

You can't decree anything into existence, because you're only a created being not the Creator. Remember the book of Isaiah in Chapter 45:9-25, can the clay say to the potter what to do, or I'm going to do this... No, only the potter can decide what and how to do it. So, if you're not God, you're not going to decree anything, period! If you say you can, it's from your own mind, not from the Bible because it's not Biblical, and certainly not factual.

Legalism is like the spirit of witchcraft, it's rebellion against the grace of God. Whoever is under Legalism is under a curse. There are only two types of people in the church: sheep or goats. You pastor or shepherd the sheep and goats, and the goats either become sheep or are taken away from the sheep.

The spirit of witchcraft (manipulation, intimidation, domination) is like cancer, either you fight it and kill it or it'll kill you. It'll destroy a church body if the leaders don't take a stand against it. False prophecy is the spirit of witchcraft; where they manipulate you for their exaltation. Prophecy is supposed to edify and comfort you. Even if the false prophet's prophecy comes true, that is still the spirit of divination because it does not exalt the name of Jesus. Until you deal with the Spirit of Witchcraft in your church, you will never be fulfilled in your commission or call.

TEACHING ON PERSEVERANCE

- Trust and obey.
- How to recognize the shame of pride.
- Can you hear the sound of revival?
- God will make a way.

We have to let the anointing of God work and do what He has ordained it to do in our lives and by faith follow the path that opens for us.

Satan will come and attack you and people will question the things you do because people won't understand God's calling on your life, but stand firm and believe the promise.

No matter what happens around you or to you, people will come against you because they won't understand your uncompromising attitude towards sin. But go on! The devil can do nothing to you because until your mission or purpose is done here on earth, God will not call you home. Don't be afraid of the devil because he is a liar, and he can't do anything to you because God has a purpose for every one of his children. So until that purpose is fulfilled you're not going anywhere. He'll try to put temptations, trials, fear, doubt, and unbelief, anything he can, but we have the victory in Jesus name, Amen! Jesus overcame the world and so must we by his glorious name! Take the example of the Apostle Paul, the devil tried to drown, starve, poison, freeze, and stone him to death. However, Paul was able to say, "I have fought the good fight, I have finished the race, and I have kept the faith" (2 Timothy 4:7).

You see, the devil has no hold on you; you have the victory in Jesus name.

TEACHING ON CHRIST'S RETURN

We better get ready for the many predictions and prophecies coming that will tell us that Jesus is coming on this day or in that year. Many so-called sincere Godly leaders, prophets and ministers are writing books or have written books saying when Jesus is coming.

Brethren, I'm telling you that is very foolish and dangerous. They are being deceived by lying spirits from Hell to confuse and to turn Christians (2 Thessalonians 2:11) away from the Lord. In the word of almighty God, he says no man will know not even the angels nor the son. (Matthew 24:36). So don't get caught up in this lying doctrine. God wants us to be watchful and to be ready when he does come, but he didn't say we were going to know when, he says the opposite. (Matthew 24:23-27; Matt 23:44.) Now regarding prophecy or a prophet, it must come to pass, but also measure up to the word of God. If not, you must reject it (Deuteronomy 13:1-5).

Jesus wants us to be ready when He comes because He will come when we do not expect Him. That's in my Bible, not the date, but his return for his bride. If we knew when He would come we would be so at ease and comfortable we would fall so low, that when He did come we wouldn't be ready anyway. We have to be obedient and walking in the spirit to be ready when He comes because every day we have to be ready.

That's why we don't know, because we would be too at ease, saying don't worry if we sinned because we can repent today, and be ready when He comes tomorrow. Can you not see what the spirit is saying to us? It would be like a compromising Christian taking our salvation for granted paying with our sins, then making a false confession to God then doing it again the next day, lying to the face of God. Brethren, now do you see in the spirit that God does things His way in His time for His Glory. In Isaiah 55:8-9, look what He says Himself! That says it all doesn't it?

Let's stop trying to outsmart God because it will never happen. Let's just live for Jesus today, walking in holiness and be ready when He comes. Amen!

Written 8/3/88

TEACHING ON DYING TO THE WORLD

It doesn't matter what happens to me --- that's what Shadrach, Meshach, Abednego, Paul and Peter said.
Why? Because, they were crucified with Christ. They were dead men, they died in Christ and rose with Him. They were dead men because dead men can't be hurt!

Do you hear what the Spirit is saying to you? People may be telling you you're nobody, you'll never be or amount to anything, you're too young, you don't speak well, but God may be allowing that so that you can be free from what others think or say about you. We need to be free from the world's hold on us, so we can minister without bondages.

If we die to the world, nothing can hurt us. If we allow God to reign over us, we will be free to minister no matter what the cost is to us physically. We must surrender all of our being to God. No, you won't be a puppet or brainwashed, you'll still be free to choose good and evil, but if you surrender all, you won't be afraid of what will happen to you in this world because there's a better place waiting for you.

TEACHING ON RELIGIOUS BLINDNESS

The hand of Providence is guiding us on our way or in our faith journey, no matter what choice you make good or bad. There's a song by Michael W. Smith called "Secret Ambition." It's about Jesus' mission to redeem us, but the religious people couldn't see it. There's a sentence in the song that gives you an idea how the religious people could be threatened. It says, "They were threatened by the voice of the 'Paragon' and His (Jesus) love wore no disguise." Paragon: 1) A model or pattern of excellence. 2) Peerless example: the paragon -- excellence of virtue. 3) To sharpen against, to compare.

Interesting, since you know the religious leaders could see something about Jesus, yet still developed hatred because it was something that was missing from their lives. They could see the love and freedom that encamped about Him. Example of getting a gift: It's free, even if you choose to leave it or walk away from it, it still is there and it's yours.

TEACHING ON THANKSGIVING: WHERE ARE THE OTHER NINE?

Luke 17:12 – 16
Verse 11: The miracle of cleansing took place during the act of faith.

Verse 12: According to the Mosaic Law, leprosy was a physical symbol of uncleanliness (Leviticus 13:12-14), the leapers as you see, called out from a distance. Why? Lepers were commanded in the law to keep away from the rest of the population (Leviticus 13:45-46; Numbers 5:2-3). The exact distance varied, but it was believed to be around 100 paces away from the people.

Verse 13: Their request was merely for mercy. They also addressed Jesus as "Master". A fairly rare word in the New Testament, used only in the Gospel of Luke and applied to Jesus. Master means, "The one who stands over", thus it implies one with authority, it's a respectful form of address. I know some may say maybe they just said Master so he would heal them and did not mean it in a respectful way. But these men must have heard testimonies from people that had been healed or actually seen Him heal so they knew He had authority."

Verse 14: Jesus tells them to go to the priest. Why? Because it was to be verified by the priest according to the law to be cleansed. Then they would be reinstated into the community. Well, if you were a leper you were considered legally dead and were no longer part of the congregation of God's people. That's why they needed approval to be restored because they were officially dead even though they were alive. Jesus also tells them, go even though you aren't healed yet and get verification (showing it is by faith, not by sight).

Was it logical to go, even though they hadn't received the healing? No, but was it logical for Moses to raise his staff at the Red Sea? Was it logical for Naaman to dip seven times in the river? Was it logical for Paul to abandon the law and embrace Grace? Faith is -- I need this -- I don't have it, and what I have isn't enough to accomplish it, so I have to trust in someone to do it for me (Christ). Because even though ten were healed only one returned to give thanks.

Verse 15, 16: A Samaritan was the only one to return, by the implication, the other nine were probably Jewish. The Samaritans were decedents from the people left in Palestine when the Northern Kingdom of Israel was subdued by the Assyrians in 722 B.C. Then they intermarried with pagans and became an outcast people. This is the man that comes back to thank a Jewish man, Jesus blesses him, showing the universal intent of the Gospel. This event, as well as, many others in the Bible demonstrated God's love for all men and any man or nationality can offer acceptable and proper praise and worship to God. What do we see in these verses?

1) Grateful, Thankful, Praise, Joy, a new beginning (like a newness of life).

2) You also see Prejudice, Pride, and Desperation.

Jews and Samaritans didn't even want to associate with each other. You could see this in other Gospel accounts. You would hear someone asking Christ, "What are you doing with that Samaritan?" In this account it's totally different, the Samaritans and the Jews were together. Why? Leprosy broke down the social barriers between them. Hey, no one wanted them around so they had to learn to live and talk with each other because of the Leprosy. Our thankfulness should be offered to Christ in our private worship and in public worship. Why? Because Jesus set the example for us.

What do we have to thank Him for?

For His goodness and mercy. For our home, our food, our family, and our church body. For His deliverance from sin and death. For His promises. For His blessings. For healing as well as sufferings. For our very life.

Written 7/18/93

TEACHING ON HINDRANCES FOR FUNCTIONING IN MINISTRY

1. Fear;
2. Lack of information, as to what God is expecting and how to operate in the gifts;
3. Misunderstanding regarding the meaning of ministry. Minister in Greek is "diakoneo" which translates to "deacon." It means to serve in a physical or natural way. Pastors and ministers aren't the same thing. A pastor is a minister, but not all ministers are pastors. In the Old Testament minister meant "a servant attendant or aide."

4. Traditions of man have been laid in encrusting layers upon the word of God and these traditions also hinder ministry flowing as it should (Colossians 2:8; Matthew 25)

Learn to do something with what God gives you, don't hide it. God gave it to you for a reason. God wants that gift to be profitable for the servicing of His Kingdom. (John 5:19) Our ministry comes forth by:

    1. Fellowship.
    2. Approval of God
    3. Ministry is something only God can begin, develop and fulfill.

Five-Fold Ministry is given to equip you to function and to minister in your gift in the body. The five-fold ministry has frequently been called the "hand ministry." The hand is the only part of the body which can reach, touch, and minister to every other part of the body. It's the part of the body that feeds, cleans, dresses, binds up, and generally cares for the rest of the body.

Usually in a church body, only 20% of the body serves in the Church and only 5% of that are really involved in the body. God's word cannot be changed or altered for any reason. God's word is forever settled in heaven and on earth. (Psalm 119:89) If any takes away or adds from the Bible, divine judgment will follow (Revelation 22:18, Matthew 24:35, Matthew 5:18, Jeremiah 1:12).

TEACHING ON 1 JOHN 1:4:7-12
LOVE DEFINED

Verse 7: John opens with the word "beloved" or as it says in the NIV, "Friends." It is saying these are people who have experienced love; showing that they had a continual practice of love toward one another because of God's great love for them and to us. Those who know agape love, know the true meaning of God's great act in sending His son to die for us while we were yet sinners (Rom. 5:8). Love originates in God because He is love (1 John 4:16, Rom. 8:30).

God not only loved us, but he translated that love into action by sending Christ on a mission to provide propitiation (Hilasmos in the Greek), which is to nullify or avert God's wrath. Also to repair our relationship to Him forever which caused the rift (1 John 2:2, 4:10), as a way of making reconciliation with Him.

In Verse 12, John says no one has seen God. Some have been going around saying they've seen God and they got a special revelation, well that is false. Does it sound familiar with what's happening today? The goal was to be transformed to love one another with his self-giving love.

Love Essential (1 John 4:13-15): The central theme is God's love for us, made plain in Christ. If you believe in His son you will have life.

TEACHING ON HEIRS TO THE PROMISE

Heirs to the Promise (Hebrew 6:13-20; Hebrews 9:16-28); Abraham waited patiently; he went from place to place. (Genesis 13:3) Illustration of Biblical waiting: When a child goes to school for the first time with his father and his father leaves him, the child knows he has to wait on his dad. Meanwhile he's playing, learning, and eating as he waits.

True Biblical waiting is as you wait you're moving as God directs you. We're not to say, "This is where I'm stuck and so this is where I'll stay." No, we should be saying "This is where I'm now, but about tomorrow only God knows."

In Genesis 17, Abram was walking before God, waiting on God's promise. God told him I will confirm my covenant with you, but Abram was still walking in God's will. That's where faith comes in. Do we have the faith in God to trust Him to supply our needs even though we may not see the promise? Do we have trust to obey when He closes or open's a door, even though we may not see the full confirmation of the promise?

Notice Genesis 12:10, Abraham comes to the promise land, but it says there was a famine. You may say that's a contradiction, but sometimes the very place God brings us to is the place where we know our greatest need. Famine can also be, we don't have the finances, the space, the people, etc., but then He opens a door and we still want to make excuses. Either you trust in Him, or you don't. Abram became fearful of God's open door, and ran away. Maybe I heard God wrong or maybe God got it wrong. I know God opened a door, but shouldn't we wait some more to be sure? Well, either you believe and trust in God's providence, that He does everything with a purpose (Isaiah 55:11, Jeremiah 29:11)or you believe in your own mind to figure out what's best.

All through the Old Testament and New Testament you see all the instances that happened to all the people that required faith walking. That is what this chapter is all about, our faith in Christ's faithfulness. I'll show examples of Old and New Testament believers and their examples to us on what Biblical faith is. Most of this chapter will be studies on the scriptures. (Ps. 32:7-11).

Verse 7 says "You are my hiding place, you will protect me from trouble and surround me with songs of deliverance."
Faith isn't our ability to hold on to God, but simply trusting in His ability to hold on to us! What Great things would you wait for, if you knew God wouldn't fail you; if you knew that even your sins and failures would not destroy God's faithfulness to you (Romans 3)?

Note to self: Waiting teaches us to say no to self and to trusting our own abilities to overcome. Do you think it's our responsibility to provide the necessities of life for yourself and family? Such as food and clothing, etc.? Right? No, wrong! Jesus said, don't worry about those things (Matthew 6:25-34). He said, "Seek first His Kingdom and all these things would be added unto you." Yes we are to work (1 Timothy 5:8), but even that is a gift.

TEACHING ON GOD IN THE UNITED STATES

We question why God has allowed us to continue living the way America is living by taking God out of school and society, and as a nation we are living as heathens instead of a Christian Nation. Let us remember the account of Sodom Gomorrah. They were destroyed and you may say but we're a hundred times worse and we're still here. So maybe God has given up and is leaving us to live as we want. But remember, every nation that has rejected God has fallen from within, ultimately destroying itself. I believe the reason we haven't been judged fully is because of the righteous people living in and praying for this nation.

Remember Sodom and Gomorrah didn't even have ten righteous people to save the city, but the U.S. has many more righteous ones trying to help this nation. Once the righteous ones are removed, I believe all hell will literally break loose on this nation. Also, we have helped God's people in Israel. We protected them in Desert Storm with our stud missiles, but once we reject or come against Israel we'll also be in trouble even though we are a larger nation than they are.

TEACHING ON LIFTING JESUS ABOVE ALL

All of our service has no power apart from the Lord Jesus Christ; He's the one that gives us all good gifts from above. He's the one who imparts us with spiritual hunger and zeal to serve Him in whatever capacity because of His love shown to us. Many of us get so caught up in our service for the Lord, that often Jesus gets pushed aside and the 'service' becomes the all-important issue in our lives.

The service or serving God in the body of Christ isn't about us. Nor is it about the good things we do; to place too much importance on the person who's doing the service, but not truth! The important truth isn't the service or the person doing the service, but the Lord Jesus Himself, and 'Him' being preached, manifested and glorified to the fullest. When we serve we must be very careful never to become so entangled in our service that we neglect to lift up Jesus who is our glory! (Colossians 1:27).

To God the message of salvation and the service are done to glorify His son Jesus, period! Apart from His son Jesus, it has no value because Jesus is salvation. He is sanctification, He is justification, and He is life to all who receive Him (John 1:12).

1 John 5:12: God did not save us for salvation or works sake, but for the sake of His son Jesus Christ through His sacrifice and the blood He shed. We must remember this in our hearts always. Everything God did was for the glory of His son Jesus Christ. That's why apart from Christ we can do nothing of value. Salvation and what it does in our lives isn't just something common, but it's the indwelling of God in our hearts which is why God has given us eternal life and this eternal life is in His son, who is Jesus Christ (1 John 5:11).

That's why there is no middle ground in Christianity. Other religions have those middle grounds. They say there are many ways to God, but the word of God tells us in 1 John 5:12, "he who has the son has life; he who doesn't have the son of God doesn't have life." It's plain and simple, either you're on God's side or on the devil's. You choose today who you will serve (Joshua 24:15). Any of our service not grounded on the indwelling Christ has as our glorifier cannot impact God's purpose to those around us and the world.

That's why Christianity isn't a doctrine or a religion, but the knowledge of a person, Jesus Christ and Him dwelling in our hearts. Christ in you, the hope of glory (Colossians 1:27).

TEACHING ON GOD'S WORD AS OUR FOUNDATION

We need a foundational teaching and solid teaching of God's word. We must become more firmly grounded in the word. We as believers need solid teachings based on Christ's work on the cross and his matchless grace, rather than merely a show of God's power. Remember Elijah, he was looking for thunder, but God spoke to him in a still small voice (1 Kings 19:10-18). Most are overlooking the prophetic moves being fulfilled with the nation of Israel and the Jewish people. God is fulfilling His promise to Abraham and restoring the Jewish people to their homeland.

Written 12/3/90

TEACHING ON SERVING GOD ZEALOUSLY

The Zeal of God has overwhelmed my soul, it's like the song we sang Sunday morning, "The zeal of God has consumed me deep in my soul, a flaming fire that consumes me as a fire that cannot be quenched." That's how I'm (we) to minister, with life and the joy of the Lord. If the body doesn't see that from us, how do we expect them to be any different?

When I preached the sermon "The Power of the Blood," it was the first time I really let God take 100% control while ministering by His spirit and the body heard what He had to say, not I.

It's liberating just to be able to write this down, I couldn't do it before. I'm not saying that I got it or arrived because I never will, praise God, I don't have to, Jesus already arrived and rose for us. We're already redeemed! Rejoice, again I say rejoice! There are many areas that God is still dealing with me and teaching me, and as long as I'm here on earth. That will always be the case because this is our training ground and we will be learning and growing in Christ.

We must be focused on finishing our race just like the apostle Paul said at the end of his life, (2 Timothy 4). We are preaching God's grace. So what is grace? "Power beyond our ability," without Christ we are nothing! (John 15:5).

CHAPTER SIXTEEN

THE POWER OF THE BLOOD

Glimpse: David preached a sermon entitled "The Power of the Blood." As he delivered this message one Sunday morning, he was overwhelmed with emotion and as he spoke about the power of Christ's Blood. He had to pause to compose himself. With his voice trembling by the power of the Holy Spirit this young pastor delivered one of his most compelling and life-changing messages he would ever deliver.

If we could just grasp David's message on the power of Christ's blood, along with eternal redemption it would set both the believer and non-believer free forever. Below is an excerpt of that powerful message from a man of God that would soon be called home in the prime of his life.

The following pages contain an excerpt of David's message, "The Power of the Blood."

Sermon Excerpt:"The Power of the Blood"

"I was just sitting one day asking God questions about the power of His blood and I was just listening and mediating on His word when the Lord asked: "So you think you know what the blood did?"

David responds, "Yes, I know what the blood did, it saved us." The Lord replied, "Yes, it saved you, but do you know what the blood did?" David continued responding, yes and that he knew what the blood did, but then sat quietly. The Lord said, "No, the blood did more than you'll ever know, you must learn to just rest." David told the congregation, that's one thing He wants us to do here today, the whole church must just rest.

I'm grieved what is happening (it's awesome what's happening) in my body today (praise God). He's grieved because what we have done to the power of his blood. The body has just taken his blood and putting it to the level that is a common thing in our life. He said it's not a common thing in our life, but its power beyond what you can even comprehend.

Do you know what it takes for the Holy of Holies to come upon this Earth, an Earth full of corruption and sin and walk upon as a man and God? Then, go through life for 33-years, man and God, without sin in a sinful corrupt world who had totally forgotten who God was. "Do you know what it was for me to go through all these sufferings," yes, many people say, I know He was nailed upon a cross, but do you know what it was for the Holy of Holies to come upon this Earth; sinless, perfect holy God who could not have sin in his sight, to come down and be upon us to give us life? "Do you know what my blood did for you, do you know what my love is, a love that would come down from a perfect holy place, come to a corrupt place because I loved you and died for you." He said, "Do you know what the blood is?" and I just wept because of the awesomeness of God's presence.

Many people go around saying, "I'm holy, I'm going to obtain that holiness. I'm going to reach that level to touch God." No, holiness is God's presence, nothing in the whole world you can do can make you holy... nothing in the whole world.

You can save 100 people, you can minister to millions; nothing will make you holy because it is my presence where holiness lives. We just need to rest in what God has done, even us, even me, knowing the grace message and coming to understand the grace message and the Lord is still trying to break through that heart of stone. You just need to rest and listen. The whole body needs to rest and listen, the whole focus that I want for my body is to look to me. If they look to me they won't have any of these problems.

We have all these problems in our lives and all these circumstances but one thing God wants us to know, the reason for these problems is because you are looking to the Earthly problems because you're not looking heaven ward.
If we would look to Him to rest in these problems, He would take care of them.

Meanwhile we go around fighting: "I have to help, I have to do something, I can't wait any longer, it's been too long, I've been stuck in this problem, I have to do something, I have to make this move." Meanwhile God is saying, "Rest and listen, rest and listen."

All through the whole Bible, the Old Testament, you see what happens to all these men because they could not wait on God. Saul, look what happened to his life because he could not wait. He went to a witch to try to get the answer and you see the end result of his life because he could not wait and listen to the Lord. It's incredible, us, we can't even comprehend. We try to comprehend eternity and we can't because we're not eternal beings, we're finite beings. The whole body of Christ struggles with eternal redemption, and they could not come to comprehend eternal redemption, once and for all, at once.

I was reading Hebrews and was getting so blessed. I was speaking to Pastor Pedro and I was being so blessed and was looking up the Greek words, "Once and for all," and it meant, "at once." How can we fight with God about that? God wants us to know that what He has established in His word thousands/millions of years before we were even born that He has established; no man can come and say, "You have lost your salvation," because He has established something in His word that no man can negate, no man. I'm telling you, no man in this whole world can negate. He wants you to know when He says in His word, "It is finished," it is finished.

He does not say things in His word to confuse you and leave you just rolling in the wind and not knowing where you're coming from or where you're going. He says it because He meant it, not because He wants you to make up your own meaning, or find your own meaning to it.

That's what's happening to the body of Christ. Many men have good hearts and want to help people, but they have to try and find their own meaning because they don't understand what His word said about eternity. Once and for all, what the blood actually meant in our lives.

Men go around trying to bring out what eternal redemption is, yes, we have eternal redemption, but if we mess up, you lost your salvation. No, Christ never said that you lost your salvation because you messed up, two thousand years before we were even born, Christ said, "I died for you while you were yet sinners," while you were yet sinners, two thousand years before you were born. Christ came on the Earth and He went to people that were not righteous and everyone came against Him because He was hanging out with prostitutes and sinners and they said, "How dare you stay with these people you're a Rabbi, what are you doing with these people?"

Christ did not come for the so called righteous, which they were not righteous, they thought they were. Christ came for us to give us life. How could he give us life if He wasn't ministering to us?

CHAPTER SEVENTEEN

SERMON EXCERPTS

Glimpse: David continues to inspire me to keep things in perspective in my adult life and to trust that God's will be done.

David taught me baseball/sports. Uncle David was always there for us even when he was tired from work, or not feeling well. He always managed to find time to play video games with us. More importantly to pray with us and for us; a life lesson for me always! He had some unusual food habits including two particular condiments; he salted and poured loads of ketchup on his food.

--- Joshua David (David's nephew)

The following pages contain sermon excerpts written by David.

SERMON EXCERPT: LACK OF FAITH

We limit God's power because of our lack of faith. Prayer removes faith in our senses and brings us back to God's promises and His Power. A Church cannot be built without prayer because it will be a useless church.

Our prayer will avail much because we are the righteousness of God. In Christ Jesus, we have the authority to overcome the enemy; the force is God's word. When scripture says 'take it by force,' the force they are referring to means, nothing is holding revival back, just our lack of prayer.

The story of Phinehas in Numbers 25 is a picture of the salvation that Jesus gave us. Phinehas' love and zeal for God stopped the death plague. Jesus did the same thing for all mankind; He came because of His love for us and stopped the sting of death.

Written 1/10/94

Additional Scripture Reference: Joshua 1:8.

SERMON EXCERPT:
THROUGH CHRIST WE OVERCOME

No, we can't do it in and of ourselves, but in Christ we can do it, (Philemon 4:12; Zechariah 4:6) not by our power or our might, but by His Spirit. John 14 states: "If I (Jesus) go away, He will come (Holy Spirit) to give you strength to overcome."By the Holy Spirit He draws people to Him, not us! We sometimes cause people to fall away from grace because of our convictions, restrictions and laws. Legalism causes them to feel they simply can't measure up, so they don't want any part of our Christianity, or what they perceive it to be.

Only the Holy Spirit can produce a divine life. We are Christians, but still struggle with the sin nature (Rom. 7). Paul struggled, he did what he hated and what he loved he didn't do. In our own strength we still will fail, but the Spirit of God in us will set us free (John 8). It's not by might, rules, regulations, but by his Spirit (Zech. 4:6) not by our efforts or works (Rom. 8). This is from God's word and the matter is settled with His word, not mine. The trouble with us is we want to do our own thing and not allow Jesus to lead us in everything. The Spirit is the one who transforms us into His likeness (2 Corinthians 3:18).

Written 1/16/94

Additional Scripture Reference: Zechariah 4:6

SERMON EXCERPT: DEATH (THE LAW)

We have incurred a penalty for sin which is death. What sin? Any sin, even just lying, etc. Even Jesus, if taking away Calvary and His sacrifice for us, couldn't have done enough good works to atone for our sins.

The moral obligation to the law of God must be paid in one of two ways. Either I pay my own debt which means I suffer eternal death and separation for God, or God the Father supplies a substitute in my place whom He will accept in my place. Then I will be redeemed and set free.

That's why, no matter how many good things or works you do; you will never repay the debt that is owed on our behalf. Why? Because it can only be repaid by a life, period! You must have a death (or blood) which may sound harsh and not fair at first. But when you see the love and mercy which God displayed in giving His son over to death in exchange for us for all eternity once and for all, only then you can begin to understand the law of God and how merciful He is with us. Even though we deserved physical death, He has given us a way out through Jesus Christ's sacrifice on the cross and His resurrected life living in and through us.

God still does require our death, emphasizing physical death; the kind of death that requires us to die to self, so He can live His life through us.

This is very important, this will change the very way you think as a child of God (I'm speaking to Christians). Our church believes that the sin issue was dealt with and this is what we preach and we will continue to preach until Christ returns. For any who may have questions, doubts, or don't really grasp or understand what we're preaching (eternal security in Christ's sacrifice once and for all).

Let me clarify what the sacrifice did and how death paid the sacrifice: The sacrifice is a substitute for someone else's crime or sin, but the sacrifice had to be without blemish and pure. That's why our death could not provide the sacrifice. The death of the sacrifice provided a covering and atonement for someone else's crime and sins. Remember this! In the Old Testament the people sacrificed animals to receive atonement from sin, but every year they had to go back and do it all over again. Now when Christ came, He became the sacrifice and died on our behalf, so that we wouldn't have to sacrifice animals anymore. Christ not only atoned for our sins, but took them away for all time (Hebrews 6; Hewbrews 10; 1 Peter 3).

The Bible speaks about this all through the New Testament, which is why we teach that the sin issue has been dealt with, but the issue of receiving forgiveness is what many Christians struggle with.

Many believe we have to repent of our sins every time we sin, or else we will not receive forgiveness. We must understand the nature of Christ's sacrifice to understand total forgiveness. How many times did Jesus die, once?

How many times did the animals sacrificed by Old Testament priests die, once? The priest couldn't use the dead animal again to receive atonement. It was impossible, why? It had died once and could not die again for the atonement. It died once for the whole year, sacrificing the same animal year after year would put the animal through public disgrace, not to mention how heartless it would be to do such a thing. The animal sacrifice was done once and the sin issue was finished and completed for the year. They didn't have to run to God to beg for forgiveness whenever they sinned because it was atoned and covered for the year. They just had to receive and acknowledge what was done for them and move on.

Now we have Jesus and His sacrifice; His blood was spilled, He died and rose again, freeing us from eternal death and giving us eternal life, once we accept Him. Without the shedding of blood there is no forgiveness of sins (Hebrews 9:22). Jesus died once on the cross for us. We then have an eternal atonement and covering for us. Through His sacrifice we believe this, but then the issue of forgiveness can be seen as a little crazy. Many Christians say how could you say you don't have to ask for forgiveness when you sin. If they could just understand the sacrificial system they would not have to carry their sins/burdens on their shoulders all the time.

Christ died once to forgive all our sins. He shed his blood once for all our sins. He died and said "it is finished," He didn't say, I'll come back every year to die and suffer all over again for you my children. No, He said once and for all. You don't have to be afraid of not confessing your sins to God because He took care of it. He said, I'll remember their sins no more (Heb. 8:12).
Christ is our covering in heaven when we sin, all He does is show the Father His wounds and the sins are forgotten so when you sin just tell the Lord I've sinned, thank you for forgiving my sin, that's not who I am in Christ, thank you Lord and go on.
You can't bring Christ back down from heaven to suffer and die for you again on the cross. Why would you want to do that? Maybe it's because you don't really know Him. You see Him as

"Far-away God," who wants to whack you over the head with a bat when you sin. So if you see him that way you won't mind having Him suffer a little more for you because you're suffering too? The death of Jesus Christ was so powerful and so far reaching, not only did it atone for all our sins for eternity, but equips you and I with the Holy Spirit. The Holy Spirit sanctifies us and makes it possible for us to live Godly lives. In Christ Jesus, all live! So rest in what He did for you for all time!

This eliminates all hope of salvation apart from the substitutionary death of somebody (which Christ did for us). With that we have pardoned and have eternal security because of Christ's redeeming sacrificial death on our behalf. We are set free from sin and brought into life with Christ which is why the Bible says, we have been bought with a price. The price was the death of Christ, who then pardoned us fully with His resurrected life. He overcame sin and death with His sinless life.

Do we have life forever? Yes. Read Titus 1:2 and 2:11. When was life bought to us? 2 Timothy 1:9-10 and 2 Timothy 2:11-13: "Here is a trustworthy saying, 'If we died with Him, we will also live with Him. If we endure, we will also reign with Him.' " Some people read this and say, you see you can lose your salvation because of what it says in Verse 12.

However, look at it in the whole context and you'll begin to see the contradiction in that thinking. Verse 11 says, if we die with Him, we live. If we endure, we reign, but if we disown Him, He disowns us. What does this mean?

It doesn't mean we lose our salvation, but that if we reject Him, (unbelief). He rejects us, it's our choice because He provided the way for us to receive life (see verse 12.) If we are faithless, He will remain faithful for he cannot disown Himself. You see, when we receive Him, even though we may mess up, He still is faithful because He cannot disown himself!

Why does it say "Himself" and not "us?" When we receive Christ, we are one and He is our life. We were bought with a price, His Life!

1/4/92, 5:15am

Additional Scripture Reference:
Hebrews 6; Hebrews 10; 1 Peter 3.

SERMON EXCERPT: IN CHRIST WE FORGE ON

We are on a journey and Christ is our guide. We have to put total dependence on Him to lead us through this life. In Christ we can go on through. (Philemon 4:13).

I was listening to a song, "Christ will Fight for our Release." Some say that may be speaking about salvation, but with salvation and grace comes the release of the law and works.

Another song says "Christ is the glory and the lifter of my head, He's my helper in times of trouble and He gives me strength in every way..."

CHAPTER EIGHTEEN

JOURNAL ENTRIES

Glimpse: Not many people can say that their cousin was also their best friend, but with David Chaluisan, I can. As kids, David and I would play sports most of the time we spent together. We both shared that love for sports. When we were together, we either collected baseball cards or played around outside. Normally, people hate Mondays, but I loved them! I only loved them because my uncle would bring David over so we could hang out. I always looked forward to them. We knew we were going to have a great time.

As teenagers, we did all the same things as when we were children. We played for St. Peters Church softball team. At that time in my life I realized that David's true love was serving God. When we were at Bible study, he would light up and answer every question that was asked. He would also relate almost everything back to the Bible. If we were watching TV, and something reminded him of a Bible verse he would not hesitate to share it.

In 1995, David stayed with my wife and I, which I can remember like it was yesterday. The two months he stayed with us were

*similar to the time we spent as kids. We would stay up late remi-
niscing about our childhood. One of our most loved subjects was
discussing our obsession with all things baseball. Of course, he
loved to bring up scripture in our conversations. It would make
them more interesting. If I had questions, he would answer them
in no time.*

*On a Sunday night in March of 1996 I got the call that David
earned his wings. My cousin called me, saying David passed
away in his sleep. I was heartbroken; it felt as if the other half
of me died with him. Until this day, when my phone rings, I get
a little nervous feeling inside. But I know that David is happy
where he is right now. David had such a major impact on my life
that I named my son after him. He showed me to keep God close
to your heart and he will not let you down!*
--- Danny Nunez (David's Cousin)

The following pages contain journal entries written by David as
he reflected on the culture of his age and his own spiritual growth
journey.

JOURNAL ENTRY: 10/31/90, 11:33pm

As I sit here writing this night, the evil activity is so rampant. We
find ourselves in the midst of a possible war in the Middle East
with a demon possessed man who claims to be the reincarnate of
King Nebuchadnezzar of the Babylon of old.

Many of our young people are dying daily from drugs, alcohol,
AIDS, suicide, and murder, etc.: 6 to 14 young people die daily
from committing suicide, over 50,000 people die yearly of drunk
driving accidents and most are young people.

Many are dying of AIDS and other related diseases and many of
our young people are sexually active. Over 70% of our young
people are having sexual relations and many of them become

pregnant and then have abortions. Over a million babies are killed a year in abortions. Millions are into new age, occult and eastern religions. Others are being abused sexually, physically, and murdered. Many young people are killing and sacrificing animals and human babies, as well as, adults for fun and supposedly for power.

Our schools are almost out of control, young kids are packing guns, killing people, selling drugs and running neighborhoods with gangs and force. What's happening to our country and our cities?

Additional Scripture Reference: Acts 17:26

JOURNAL ENTRY, 3/4-6/1987

I know there is a purpose for me coming on this retreat in upstate New York. The Lord does things just at the right time. It's wonderful the way He does things, we just have to stand in awe of His mighty hand at work. Heb. 12:28-29

Day 1 of Fast – I tell myself I'll fast one day to pray, study, and read His word. God has something else in store for me. I get up early in the morning and start my spiritual retreat, and communion with God in the beautiful countryside and mountains of upstate New York in the town of Pottersville. Up here you see the majesty and wonderful work of creation in the lakes, hills, and the whole countryside. It's so clean, innocent, and quiet. You can hear God speaking to you in a great and mighty way. He's telling you, 'Look at My handy work and My creation.

Take a deep breath and smell it and then tell Me I'm not present and I'm a weak God, as many Christians express, not with their mouth, but inwardly with their hearts and their spirit by not believing in me fully with all their hearts." They fear evil (devil) more than me by letting Satan put fear in their lives and not rebuking and resisting him and demanding him to get out of their lives 2 Timothy 1:7. God didn't give us a spirit of fear, but of power, love and discipline.

Why are we like this? It's so simple. If we would do what He told us to do, we would not mask our fear and lie to God and everyone we know. Fear is not confessing to God wholeheartedly, maybe He'll deliver us from that sin, but then He'll send us to Africa to be missionaries.

That's why most of us are defeated. We lie to God's face and we expect Him to work fully in our lives because of fear of what will happen in our lives. We are powerless Christians. We are lying to God, and the devil is lying to us by putting even more crazy and fearful thoughts in our heart. When we stop lying to God, we stop giving the devil a foothold and leaving ourselves open to lying spirits who try and hatch evil and fearful thoughts in our lives.

So next time you say, why am I like this? Go to God and He can reveal the truth to you. Go wholeheartedly and you will see the difference when you allow Him to have full control of your life. (Matt 6:33).

Unbelief is worldliness and lack of faith. When we don't believe God because we are only seeing some of His work, we don't allow Him to work in our lives because we love the world more than Him and are holding earthly things too tightly. Our unbelief stems from our minds being closed and blinded to the things and work of God by our own actions. God cannot work in our lives if we don't believe in His power, love, and discipline!

JOURNAL ENTRY, DATE UNKNOWN, 11:37pm

Subject: World prophetic events unfolding in our times.

I sit here and watch the ABC Nightly News and hear what is going on over the whole European World. The Lord continues to confirm what I've seen. The Soviets have a large stock of chemical weapons. They were just transporting chemicals to a certain location, and they were photographed doing it, but denied it as always.

Iraq used chemical weapons on their own people. The people that weren't killed by the bomb were killed by inhaling the chemicals. The witnesses say it was different colors and didn't rise very high then it evaporated, but some of the people and children were blinded by it. It was not a nice thing to see people lying dead in the streets. Syria is now trying to establish means of making chemical weapons. The nations are now having a convention to destroy and disband chemicals weapons. Everyone is arguing about this, but no one will disband their own weapons so it's really a waste of time. Peace, but there is no peace. The signs of the times are starting to spring up in silent ways to the natural eye (man). But to the spiritual man (eyes), they are the beginning of birth pains.

God's unconditional judgment prophecies operate on a similar principle. The repentance of an individual or a generation may postpone such a prophecy, but it cannot cancel it. Some prophecies are not always fulfilled and some prophecies are conditional with their fulfillment dependent on human behavior. Others are unconditional and will take place no matter what else happens. Conditional prophecy depends upon our obedience. If we disobey, personal prophecy will be annulled by our own actions. You can see the ministry of Saul in the Old Testament (1 Samuel 13:13-15 and 1 Samuel 9:15- 10:8).

Rebellion against a prophetic word, Samuel said, is like the sin of witchcraft. Stubbornness in not following a prophetic word exactly is iniquity and idolatry. (1 Samuel 15:23). Clearly, then, personal prophecies require faith to fulfill and obedience to obtain.

JOURNAL ENTRY, 1/12/93

As I sit here in my sister's kitchen at 12:30am, I am being blessed with God's spirit. I've been reading for close to two hours and praying about the situations in my life. Knowing changes have come, but more are coming and not fully knowing how to express myself except through my writing. Maybe God will use me in that way. I'm beginning to see God opening doors for our small church body leading to a new place to worship and knowing its God's leading, but at the same time I find myself troubled by some of the member's responses.

During this time in my life I find the Lord is doing a tremendous spiritual teaching in my heart. As a young minister my personality is different from the head pastor. He's more outspoken and I'm more quiet and laid back. I don't want to step on anyone's toes and I'm trying to please them and not bring them down, thinking that's God's will so we can build them up.

But the last couple of weeks the Lord has been teaching me to let Him do the talking and the body will receive life instead of boredom. We have a liberating message of life from God to share with everyone. His grace shed upon us through Jesus Christ. We all claim to know the full grace message of God's unconditional love, God's unconditional acceptance and God's unconditional provision concerning our salvation. Yet we live and act like we have a common thing.

As I write this I weep and grieve, but also with the joy of the Lord purging through me like a river of living water. Why grieve? I grieve because I have preached until recently from my own thoughts intermingled with God's spirit. I have preached many times like I haven't crossed over from death to life. My brothers and sisters in Christ, we have crossed over from death to life, forever! Where is our trust in God which we claim to have? Where is the joy that should be pouring out from the very fibers of our being in knowing that the creator of the whole universe lives in us?

We panic because we don't know fully what God is doing, but praise God we don't because we're not supposed to know God's every move. If we did we wouldn't understand anyway because we can't even understand what's happening now. How are we going to understand what is to come?

Beloved God never promised us freedom from hardships (1 Pet 4; 5). Look at how God answered Job. God never answered his questions with answers, but answered him with His majesty and power (Job 37-42). Job had to rest in God's providence in knowing God had everything under control, even though he was suffering for no apparent reason.

If you read the whole account of Job's life you see how God blessed him even more at the end of all his sufferings. One characteristic of Job which may apply to us is our ego and/or pride. We think we're righteous in and of ourselves, and then we suffer and get angry at God. We let our pain become our whole world, whatever you may be going through. I know there are situations that are very painful to even talk about and it's not easy to go on and not give up. We have to get out of our self-pity and see there's a big world out there bigger than ourselves and understand God rules it with justice and love.

We wonder, *How? I'm suffering; I've got cancer, AIDS, etc.*

Well, if God allows that in your life, remember God isn't the author of sickness and evil, but sin caused suffering to fall on us all, good or bad. He has a greater purpose for you and He will work it out for good (Romans 8:28). Remember that if God can manage this troubled world, He can manage your trials. If we could see all the people that are facing the same trials, we might understand that everything we have here on earth is just a gift and a privilege. We too might say, like Job, "Naked I came and naked I shall depart, the Lord gave and He took away" (Job 1:21.) When we die we have to remember that we aren't taking anything with us. We have to understand that we have no right to protest to God about losing anything, but we still do, why shouldn't we? Because anything we had "wasn't ours to begin with" (1 Timothy 6:7.) We always seem to think that we have certain rights as a believer: the right to be happy, for good health and blessings. There is nothing wrong with that, but that's not what being a Christian is about because if these things were gone, would you be angry and lose your faith in God? Then, we have to understand that we have no rights to anything on this earth, which is of no eternal value.

You may disagree with me, but that's what the Bible teaches. Jesus said, "Put me first and all the rest will follow, and don't worry about tomorrow and what you will eat or drink for I feed even the sparrow." In 1 Tim. 6:7-8, the Bible says "For we brought nothing into the world, and we take nothing out of it, but if we have food and clothing, we will be content with that."

When we realize that everything is a gift; there comes into our lives a joyful gratitude for what God has given us, even for the things we don't have. We're not looking for material things, but we're looking to God to supply our needs. As the apostle Paul said, "I'm content in whatever circumstance, I know what it is to be in need and what it is to have plenty. I've learned to be content in any and every situation, whether well fed or hungry, whether living in plenty or want." Why was he so content? With Christ He could go through all things and Christ gave him the strength to carry on his mission (Philemon 4:11-13).

1 Timothy 6:9 says people who want to get rich fall into traps and into many temptations from foolish and harmful desires that plunge men into ruin and destruction. We have to be careful where our heart is and allow Jesus to guide us in every decision

we make (Matthew 6:19-24). When I have allowed God to take control and put it in His hands, whatever the situation, I always receive a joy that overwhelms my soul. It's like the song: "The Zeal of God has consumed me, deep in my soul, a flaming fire that consumes me, a fire that cannot be quenched." That's how we are to live, and to minister; with life and joy in the Lord. If people don't see that from us, how do we expect them to be any different? Don't be fearful if that's not what you're experiencing at this moment. Just continue praying and walking by faith in God's promises and you will see the Lord open doors that will surprise you!

There are still areas in my life where God is still teaching me and as long as I'm here on earth that will be the case. This here and now is our training ground and we will always be learning and growing in the knowledge of Christ and His image until we finish the race just like the apostle Paul did.

Additional Scripture Reference: 2 Timothy 4.

Letter to Christ for Nations Bible College

I received Jesus Christ as my personal savior when I was 10-years-old. I was attending my church, The Mission, on a Friday night service, to see a film about how Jesus changed the lives of many people who had received Him as Lord and Savior in their lives.

The film also showed what happened to people who had rejected Jesus and continued in their worldly way of living. All it brought was death and destruction to the person's life. There was no real joy, peace, and happiness in their life because something was missing, that was Jesus.

That night I gave my life to Jesus when the alter call was made. I now found what I was missing in my life: Jesus. I continued to try to live the way Jesus said in his Word, but I didn't have a good study time in the Word. I would forget to read the Word or pray. We moved away so we stopped going to that church and I quickly forgot my commitment to Christ.

When I was 13 years old I began attending a Lutheran church in my new neighborhood. I got involved in the youth ministry and continued to grow in the Lord mostly through the youth group, but also through my own studies at home. I was growing in knowledge of the Word, but my spiritual life was drifting away from God and I started to see it for the first time. The Lord began his work in me showing me what I had said when I was in that little church. He showed me the condition I was in spiritually.

What is happening to many churches today is they grow in head knowledge but their hearts are far away from God. That is what was happening to me, and the Lord began working in me so I could change that and begin to grow spiritually.

I knew that something was missing in my walk with God. He said in His word we shall receive power when the Holy Spirit has come upon us (Acts 1:8.) When I was 16 years old I attended a crusade and rededicated my life to Jesus. A few weeks before that I had a dream of the world ending; I was not going with Jesus in the rapture because of my disobedient heart and life towards him. When I awoke I knew I had to change, which started my whole new life with Jesus.

In 1986, I received the baptism in the Holy Spirit and it has changed me in wonderful ways knowing that Acts 1:8 is true and it is for today. That's what was missing in my life: power from above. That I now see. The scales have fallen off my eyes and I now have a new hunger and zeal for God.

In 1988, I left the Lutheran Church by the leading of the Holy Spirit and started attending Times Square Church. There I have learned about holiness, grace and also the judgments of God. I continued to grow in the word and about the prophetic ministry being restored today.

The Lord continues to break me, mold me, and take me through refining fire to make me a clean, holy man of God willing to sacrifice all for Him and His work. I desire to attend Christ for the Nations Bible College because I believe that God is leading me into ministry. Your Institute has been a great blessing and help in my life. I received your magazine through the mail and I've been praying about going to Bible College.

The Lord has been ministering to me that it's time to move on with him, that I have to get ready to get involved in the spiritual war that is going on in the world because the time is close to his coming. I sent for information on your correspondence course from Dallas, Texas. Their response was to watch and pray for God's answer. I continued to write for a catalog. I received yours in the end of January.

In Jesus,
David Chaluisan, Jr.

JOURNAL ENTRY, 9/2/90

As I sit here this night in my room alone, there is a storm outside with powerful thunder and lightning all around. I'm listening to Christian artist, Steve Camp's "Living Dangerously in the Hands of God," and the lyrics say "our Lord, He is a hiding place, His hold is strong and sure, though the storms may rage around me, and in His love I stand secure." (2 Corinthians 1:6-9) What a wonderful song because it demonstrates just what our Lord is like – He is powerful and just, but also wonderfully merciful to us, keeping us safe and always watching us, keeping His hand around us.

That's why we can all stand secure, no matter what the situation, good or bad, because either way we are free from the death and destruction that surrounds us. So we all must learn to rejoice and be glad in everything and in every situation that confronts us, strong and secure! We have the Creator of the Universe on our side. If we obey Him (Jesus) and follow His word (Bible) with all our hearts we will have victory. If God is for us who can be against us (Romans 8:31). That doesn't mean we won't have trails, temptations, persecution, sickness and hardships because brothers and sisters in Christ we all will sooner or later. We all will have confrontations with evil, but we must learn to overcome in the name of Jesus our Lord and Savior.

In the past year, since 1989, many things have happened to me that can make you want to question what the Lord is doing in our lives; I'm 23 years old right now, a young man.

On November 13, 1989, around 7:40pm, I was taking my sister and my two nephews to the hospital because my nephew Nicky (one year old) had a fever. While on the way there a car making an illegal left turn hit us and dragged us sideways. Before I could even see him he hit us. We were hit in the front and my side was hit first, but thank God we were all fine except for some bruises and cuts. I also suffered back pain and my glasses broke. The car was totaled and we were all fine.

You might say it is because the Lord kept us from harm's way. We all got up and walked away from the accident, but the way we were hit would make you thankful as well. The driver of the other car was going around 50 miles per hour and our car took most of the impact. I had my sister and her baby in front seat without a car seat because it was my father's car. A police officer said that if I had been in another car we probably would not have survived or had been pinned in the car. I was driving a 1979 Audi 5000S, but a couple of months earlier I was driving a Datsun 210, a small car which the police officer and other people around said if I still had we probably would have been dead. The Datsun broke down about a month or two before, so my father bought the Audi from my cousin whom he had not seen for many years until a family reunion. So, you see, God has His ways, and we sometimes will not understand them, but we have to trust Him because he knows what's best for us.

Then on July 29, 1990 my first car was stolen right in front of my house. Ten days later the police found the car with which appeared to have been involved in a crash on the front and side. The ones who stole it were teenagers, 12 and 15 years old ,along with two others. They had been caught the same day they stole it after the crash.

Many things will happen that we will not understand (1 Corinthians 13:12), but we have to keep moving on. God does not want us to seek material or worldly things, those things are temporal. He wants us to seek spiritual things. Things like cars, jewelry, etc. are fine; the danger begins when these things take your heart away from following Him and He is not first, that's when there is danger. For where your heart is, there also will be your treasure (Luke 12:34, Matt. 6:19-21, Luke 6:45). Read this over and over and let the Holy Spirit speak to you and teach you what this means.

I've experienced many trials and have battled various ailments since I can remember; rheumatism, scarlet fever, and paralysis. I'm the only son born to my parents. I have five sisters. My mother had a miscarriage a year before I was born, it was a boy, and she lost her daughter at 15 years old. She was killed and my mother was pregnant with me at the time of my sister's death. Due to my mother's condition, I almost died during birth. We will have times of great blessings, but also will have sufferings, it's in the Bible (1 Peter 4:12-19).

I could go on and on about all the things that have happened to me and I know that God has had his hand on me, keeping me safe. If you look back you will see times when He has kept you safe and out of harm's way.

I remember driving my car from Queens to Staten Island. The middle of the tire was completely ripped away and only the thread of the tire was left in the middle. I didn't know until I got home and my father showed me. It ripped while I was driving on the highway. I heard something and stopped, but didn't see anything so I kept on driving. When I saw it I was amazed. I still thank God for that one.

Another time, I was walking to school with my father when I was 7 years old. I was late to school that day so my father was rushing to get me there. As we were walking to school which was about five city blocks away, my father decided to go into a store. I think it was an auto store or hardware store.

All of a sudden we heard a loud noise and crash outside. We ran outside and there was a car on top of a light post on the sidewalk. Witnesses say that after we had walked into the store, the car came right on the sidewalk where we were walking and drove on the sidewalk down the whole block before crashing into the light post at the end of the block. He was either drunk or had a heart attack, I don't remember, but the man that saw it, said if we had not gone into the store at that moment we would have been killed. Tell me that wasn't God's divine protection because I know it was Him keeping us from harm's way.

God has a purpose for all of us! If we choose to follow Him we will fulfill our purpose in the time He gives us! So don't worry about what you're going to do for God, keep on praying and one day He will show you and you will know, even if it means to be a servant to others or to save someone's life, physically and spiritually. Do not worry because you won't die until God's will is done in your life so do not fear the devil.

If you disobey and turn and reject God then your life is no longer in God's protective arms and you have taken your life in your own hands. A bad place to be because without God we can do nothing of eternal value. You will then reap what you sow; if you sow to the carnal nature you will reap worldly things that bring death and destruction, but if you sow spiritual things you will reap spiritual (good) things that are eternal.

Additional Scripture Reference: Romans 2:6-8, Romans 8:5-17, Galatians 6

CHAPTER NINETEEN

<u>BOOK EXCERPTS</u>

Glimpse: I can't say I have many distinct memories of my Uncle David, but working on this book and helping paint his story really taught me about the man behind the glasses.

I have heard stories about his amazing faith and love for God and family, but after reading through countless passages of his work, I see there was so much more. Behind this humble, meek, and mostly shy man, lived a ferocious lion-like passion for the Word of God. His vision was the Great Commission, which is to spread the words of Jesus all across the globe. Unfortunately, he was not able to fulfill those goals, but like his Savior that he proclaimed, he left behind some notes and words for us to learn and spread. David's writings are an accumulation of poems, songs, prophecies, dreams, and devotions.

Within these writings are intimate details of his relationship with Jesus, and also his keen sense to observe the world around him and its smaller details.

I see a little bit of David in each of us (family), and I believe it is because of the importance he felt it was to leave an impact on our lives while he had time on this Earth. The first immediate impact I can think of is the salvation of his family. It was David's persistence and yearning to be close to the Lord that then in turn got his parents and sisters, and eventually their children saved. When he was pastoring his church he was able to teach and lead his entire family.

Those are actually my first memories of him. I remember sitting in the church and having stuff for kids passed around as me and Nick sat through the service preoccupied with the Fruit Stripe Gum coloring books as he spoke.

David brought my mother and I to our first church outside of his as well, Calvary Assemblies of God. I remember walking in on a Wednesday night at about 5-years-old. He knew the pastor, and assured us it was a good church.

I vaguely remember his room in the Brooklyn house, and even more vaguely him living with us on his little futon bed in the basement next to his stationed typewriter. I also remember him more distinctly having the little room at the Olivo house.

When David moved to Florida, the wandering boy finally went home. He had the room across from Titi Becky's, and boy were they distinct from each other. Becky's room was filled with girly stuff and bright colors, and David's, with sports memorabilia, comic books, baseball cards, and notebooks everywhere. Some contents of the room included a Roberto Clemente baseball card plaque, a Jets lamp, some posters on the closet door, an eagle frame, and a picture I drew for him on the wall.

Unfortunately I did not share the passion for sports so I can't recall any catches or games watched, but I do remember the time we played basketball in the driveway. I remember watching wrestling with David and my grandfather while we ate cookies, and of course dancing around to Carman and DC Talk. I have often wondered what he would think of my music, and the stuff I listen to now.

He and Grandpa also took me to my first baseball game along with Jr, Josh, and Nick, and we took an infamous trip to the Baseball Hall of Fame that kind of went well...

I recall parts of the long conversation we had the night I gave him the drawing mentioned, and when he said, "This will never leave my wall," probably the only promise he ever broke, and through no fault of his own. I would do anything to see that picture again wherever it is.

I have memories of waking up at 9:00 a.m. to talk about the Bible with grandpa as David was getting home from work. He would come in, eat a Hot Pocket, fry a piece of Salami, and throw a pile of salt on everything including a sandwich. He loved his salt almost as much as he loved saying, "I don't know how I do it, I just a-do-it," "Salami Con Bacon," (a delicacy in his head), and the scary "Evil Ernie" who was always out to get us, but just never did.

I believe my last memory with David was going to the .99 cent store and him buying a few things. It was there he got me these little red and yellow robots and a coloring book. We then hopped into his little car, which I distinctly remember had to be locked manually. The seat belts where in two; first you wrapped the bottom, and then you brought the top across. I still have those robots and coloring book by the way.

Lastly, I remember the dreaded phone call that shook me from my sleep when I heard my mother scream out. That is a haunting sound that I will never ever forget. I wrestled with writing about this, but this is the full story, this is full circle, and this was a family unit.

Together, all of us: Sarachiks, Logozzos, and Olivos all flew to-gether on the same plane, all rented cars, and all drove to Ocala from Orlando. A lot of other family members were there as well, and we were all able to grieve together which in the end let Da-vid do something else, bring the family together one more time to wish him goodbye.

I regret being too young to really have any kind of emotion and take full grasp of what was happening. I was able to hear "Big House" by Audio Adrenaline, and I went to McDonald's Play Place with Uncle Danny and Nick. Looking back I am almost upset with how little I remember the funeral or being sad. It was just me being a kid I guess, and now in reliving the past, writing this, and thinking of Julie's letter, that a flood of emotion made parts of this book unbearably difficult to read. I guess it is me grieving the way I should have all these years later. Knowing what I know now, I know that this loss would have been devas-tating to me as a 25-year-old, even a 16-year-old, my age when I lost my grandfather.

This brings me to my final point, and something my cousin Dan-ny, perhaps David's closest family member, outside of his immedi-ate family, said to me at my grandpa's funeral. He said something to the effect of, "Aside from David, your grandfather was the best person I ever knew in terms of character. Neither of them ever had a bad word to say about anyone, and I can't think of anything they wouldn't do for someone else."

Thinking about this now, the little memories I have of David, I was able to experience with my grandpa. They were one in the same, David Sr. and David Jr. They both loved like no one else, and instilled that love of God and family to everyone around them. They loved baseball and the Mets, and cherished the indi-vidual time with us. Knowing my grandfather means I knew my uncle because everything my grandpa imparted on me, he im-parted on his son first.

Uncle David, I did not get to know you as much as some of my cousins, but it is evident the importance you have had on my life. I thank you for the memories I do have, and I look forward to the day we meet in Heaven again. We can field our own ball club; Olivo brothers in the outfield, Kayla and I up the middle at Shortstop and Second, Ralphy and Danny at 1st and 3rd, and you and grandpa at catcher and pitcher. Just keep your arms warm.

> *---Justin Sarachik (David's nephew)*

The following pages contain ideas, concepts, written fragments and whole chapters of books that David aspired to complete and publish.

BOOK EXCERPT: FAITH WALKING

A well-known televangelist said "Faith is temporary for every transaction and is not forever." Temporary faith? You have to keep receiving new faith because it'll fade for various reasons or situations? If that's the kind of faith you have, then it's not faith at all!

In Luke 17:5-6, the disciples asked God to increase their faith, but Jesus said, "If you have faith as a mustard seed, you can say to this Mulberry tree be uprooted and it will obey you." You can't increase your faith in your faith because it'll do you no good because you, in yourself, can do nothing (John 15:5). But if you have faith in Jesus, even if it's as small as a mustard seed, you can move a tree, a mountain, anything. Why? Because notice how Jesus answers them. He didn't say, I'll give you more faith in your faith, no. He said if you have faith, what kind of faith? Faith in His faithfulness, knowing that with Him guiding you and fighting for you, you can do anything! Even if your faith in Him is as small as mustard seed; He is the one who's a big God who can do anything through us if we trust and have faith in Him to accomplish it (1 Kings 22:5).

Proverbs 20:18 states: "Make plans by seeking advice; if you wage war, obtain guidance." Faith walking is total dependence on Christ and His will being done in your life. You see, if you don't seek advice which is advice from the Lord, you can do nothing. Your plans will always end up causing disappointment and confusion. Why? Because without advice and guidance from the Holy Spirit you will always fail, either sooner or later. Without spiritual wisdom, you are doing it with your own human wisdom and as you can see, from previous chapters, what happened to Saul and even David (1 Samuel 28, 2 Samuel 11) because of their human wisdom.

Scripture Reference: Hebrews 11: Enoch (vs. 4); Abraham (vs. 8-19); Noah (vs. 7); Moses (vs. 23-29); Isaac (vs. 20); Jacob (vs. 21); Joseph (vs. 22); Rahab (vs. 31); Gideon, Barak, Samson, Jephthah, David, Samuel (vs. 32); The Prophets (vs. 33 - 40).

BOOK EXCERPT: DANIEL

Daniel (God is my judge) also called (Belteshazzar); the Hebrew servant and prophet at Babylon.

Daniel was carried away as a captive to Babylon when he was about 16-years-old. He was from a Jewish family of high rank and youth of fine promise. He was chosen together with some other Jewish young men for special training at Nebuchadnezzar's Court.

Being a young man of strong convictions and courageous independence, he was able to withstand the temptations of an ungodly environment.Demonstrating remarkable qualities of intellectuality, wisdom, and leadership, he rose to the highest political position under the king and retained a place of very high authority in the median and Persian empires which in turn succeeded the Babylonians.

Prophet Daniel saw and interpreted remarkable visions. Although he didn't himself return to Jerusalem he had the joy of seeing the

Babylonian captivity come to an end under Darius, King of Persia and some 50,000 of his fellow countrymen return to their beloved land. His political and prophetical activity extended over a period of 70 years. The twelve chapters of Daniel fall naturally into two divisions.

The first six chapters are of events in the life of Daniel, the last six chapters are an account of four great visions. The central thought of the whole book: "The Sovereignty of God."

Editor's Note: I read the next book excerpt at David's wake, I felt it was life imitating art, or was it?

BOOK EXCERPT: AKA (REVELATION) - A NOVEL

Chapter 1

Day 1 from my Journal: My name is David and I'm writing these notes to remind myself of the words spoken to me and given to me concerning the closing of the age. Bare with me as I write in my journal. As you read on you'll begin to understand what I'm writing about. It may seem too overwhelming at times and even unbelievable, but pray for understanding and spiritual eyes to see. If you're reading this journal now, it will mean that my mission is done here on earth and the Lord has called me home to glory, you'll understand more as you read.

What I now want to talk about are the special people in our midst. In society there are many special people, but who are they? Why is it that society at large only sees the outward appearance and then calls that special, beautiful, etc.? What exactly are the qualifications of a special person? For that matter what exactly is a special person? Do you have a special person living next to you? Do you even care? Society always runs to the beautiful people, the ones who look ravishing, speak well and respond well. What about the ones who don't look ravishing or speak well and respond well? Do these people even count because in our day (1994) it seems that we don't care period, and we live that way. But do these special people have qualities that are over looked because of appearances or because of being unseen, unknown and unloved? What about them makes it more special because of a gift that God may have given them that remains untapped and needs to be made known, for it to benefit man in this life and in the life to come.

They may be afraid to show or talk about it for fear of reproach or ridicule. Are they fighting in their spirit man for control of this untapped gift that needs to be cultivated for the good of man, or are they already misusing it to overpower others? Could they be using their God given gifts to prey on their own brethren? Well, I guess I'll have to find out one way or the other, that's what my mission is all about. In case you're still wondering who I am and what I'm writing about in this journal, I'll tell you a little about myself. I'm a 27- year-old who has studied for four years in a seminary and before that, four years in Bible College. I received my Doctorate in Practical Theology, but nothing that has happened to me in the last few months is practical (little did I know that I would be taken through seven years of unpractical experiences).

I'm a minister, but have no church because of the road I have chosen to follow. I'm also a born again Christian, yes, I know, in our society that's a bad word (little did I know how bad it would become for those who bear that name). But many in our society don't exactly know what that means. I've seen many different people in religious circles attempt to explain to society what being religious is all about, but I have heard few explain what it means to be born again.

Many claim to be standing for Christ, but never fully understand the person who they claim to be representing. Society feels trapped and disguised by these so called Christian people who claim God is love, but do nothing to show forth the love they claim to have. In the past many have used the word 'Christian' in society, people like Hitler, ruling religious parties in the dark ages and middle ages, the crusaders, etc. They killed in the name of Christ, but they didn't know Him or what a 'Christian' really is or they wouldn't have done what they did! They followed man-made religious traditions and were led by evil forces that controlled their thinking because they weren't Christians, hence they killed for what they thought was good, but was actually evil, and that's what 'religion' does and many times returns people into bondage.

To explain to society what being a 'Christian' means, I'll start by saying it's not being religious or having or getting religion, it's not a set of rules and regulations to man, but it's a relationship with a person, who was also God who came in the flesh to live among us and die for us because He loved us. When Jesus Christ came to this earth almost 2000 years ago, He taught us a new way of living. He did away with the written code of atoning for our sins.

Why? Because He abolished the old system of trying to maintain your atonement by keeping all the law, as many were doing, but no man could keep. We needed a perfect, holy sacrifice to set us free from our struggles from always failing to maintain the holy laws of God which no man alive could maintain. God in His wisdom had a plan in motion from the beginning of time to save us from our sin by His son Jesus Christ coming down to live with us for a while and then by His perfect life to die in our place and do away with the old system of trying to keep the law and to maintain our forgiveness. He was led to the cross to die for us and there took all our punishment on Himself and when He died, His shed blood on the cross set us free from sin and death. All we have to do is accept Him as our only way to heaven.

When we do this He becomes our Savior and we become His children and new creations in Him because His Spirit comes and lives in our hearts. We then are born again. We then have a relationship with Him, not an old dreary religious life of Do's and Don'ts. That's not to say we have no standard, but it makes us want to please Him and His ways even more and compels us to live a life of obedience to Him. We are totally forgiven by His blood once and for all, and we are then free to serve Him with total love to impact this evil society for His glory. That's the true nature of Christianity.

I have been entrusted with a special task. First I must preach the good news of Jesus Christ to all I can, then I must find these others, set aside special people in the USA and around the world with these special endowed gifts, not only to help society physically, but spiritually. To begin my journey I must find them first. Yes, I know you have questions, I do too; the Lord Jesus Christ appeared to me and gave me a mandate to find these people and begin the last day harvest of the Gentiles.

I don't know why me? Why these people? But I'm learning as I go to put total trust in Him and allow Him to guide me through this mission. He showed me the spirit world and the battles that angels were fighting on our behalf to thwart the demonic attacks from the devil. Seeing this makes me feel like John in Revelation. I was completely changed by seeing this activity, my whole being began to flow with light and I felt holy power flowing to the very fibers of my being. Jesus Christ told me I would be indestructible (like a pariah watching the madness around him, but I would be able to do something about it, unlike a pariah). Jesus also told me to watch, for many of these people I seek, do not know the truth yet!

So I will have to be an evangelist and a revealer of truth to these people. There are 102* people I must find: Two from every state in America, and there are many more in other countries. I don't know how many and if I'm to go to them, or even how I'm going to find them, but find them I must, for God is with me and guiding my way.

He has given me a new name to go by when I find these people since I must be a revealer of truth to many of these. I have been given the name of Revelation.

I know this may sound too much like a comic book, but you can think of this like the greatest comic book that you will ever read, except this is real, the people are real, the forces of good and evil are real. I already know about the two people in New York, where I am from and am heading to Buffalo, New York to find the first person I'm seeking. I pray that God will lead me and give me the wisdom and grace to be able to talk and guide this person in his mission from God, so he can impact society in New York for God. My journey is just beginning; I'll continue learning as I go about my gift and the gift of the others.

BOOK EXCERPT: WINNING BATTLES AND WARS

In Chapter 1, I discussed shouting and fighting unto the Lord. In Chapter 2, I discussed overcoming storms and in this Chapter (4), I'll discuss examples of biblical characters and how they fought and won their battles and wars. The answer is simple; these examples prove to reaffirm our faith in God's faithfulness to us. What an awesome mighty God we serve! (Hebrews 11:30) Daniel, Shadrach, Meshach and Abednego.

I'll start with the story of Phinehas, one of the little known charters of the Bible, yet he played a significant role in his time because he loved the Lord with all his might, heart, soul, and strength. Phinehas was a priest and the grandson of Aaron, Moses brother. In Judges chapter 20, you see that Israel fights the Benjamites because of the evil a Levite Priest did to his concubine (read about it in Judges Chapter 19). In chapter 20:27 you see

Phinehas ministering before the Ark of the Covenant. What I love about Phinehas and this chapter is the lesson to be learned. In verse 18 you see Israel goes to inquire of the Lord and the Lord answers. For two days Israel gets beaten in the battlefields, first they lose 22,000 men then 18,000. The people of Israel were weeping, fasting, and giving burnt offerings to God because of what was happening, but Phinehas hadn't given up. In verse 28 he was still ministering before the Ark of the Covenant even after two days of losing 40,000 men. He could have given up on the war and said, "We're defeated," but it says he was still ministering. What a great example to us and to the leaders and pastor's to not give up just because it looks hopeless, but to continue to minister, rejoice, and again I say rejoice (Phil. 4:6-7).

Phinehas inquires of the Lord and God says, tomorrow I will give them into your hands and without hesitation Israel went out and even though the battle looked as gray as before, they struck down 25,000 men that day. Notice verse 35 says "the Lord defeated Benjamin before Israel," that's right we are nothing without Him (John 15:5) and the battle does belong to the Lord (Deut. 20:4 & 1 Chron. 5:20 & 22), quite an example for us! The next day the battle looked grim, but they hung tough because God was with them. They killed another 25,000 men that day and defeated the Benjamites.

The lesson here for us is this, though your battle or war may look unwinnable at the time, the Lord is with you, fighting for you, that is if you let him because many times we not only fight our very own problems, but we fight God too by not releasing the problem to Him. We need to do what He wills, for his glory! So, if you're going through a battle or war right now in your life, don't try to analyze or overcome your battle on your own. Release it to Him, and rest in His providence and His might, to win the battle for you (Zech. 4:6) because the battle belongs to the Lord. Give it to Him and you can't lose! It's Biblical, it's not my words, it's God's word. (1 Chronicles 5:20, 22).

We see Phinehas in Numbers 25 and how his zeal for the honor of God was a part of him. He went in and killed the evil Israelite worshiping Baal and committing sexual immortality with a Midianite woman who was with him in his tent; and the plague against Israel was stopped. Those who had died of the plague had numbered 24,000 and because of this, Phinehas turned God's anger away from Israel and stopped the plague. Phinehas was blessed and God made a covenant of peace with him, and his descendants would have a covenant of a lasting priesthood because he was zealous for the honor of God and made atonement for the Israelites. (Num. 25:10-13) Even though Phinehas was a leader, priest, and a prominent man, he wasn't afraid to get involved and get his hands dirty! Do you know what I mean? That's a lesson for all of us to learn.

Phinehas knew how to relate to the people, but also didn't let his position make him prideful and always relied on the Lord. In the midst of our battles and time of spiritual warfare we need to learn from Phinehas and his life and who he went to for guidance in his battles. You can read about Phinehas in Joshua 22:13-32; 1 Chronicles 9:19-20; Judges 20; 28; Numbers 31:6.

Joshua is another man God used and we can learn from. Joshua means (Jehovah, His helper). In the book of Joshua, the theme is conquest in the name of the Lord. A fitting name because that is what I'm speaking about; if God be for you, who can stand against you (Romans 8:31). Even if it seems hopeless at the present time, if God is with you, your battle and wars will pass and you'll walk right on through and conquer it in the name of the Lord. Remember that he's the one that will guide you through your battle and war, not our might or yours (Zechariah 14:6). Joshua's name was Ho-shea, it's in (Numbers 13:8, 14:30, and 16.

Hoshea meant salvation, but God was showing Joshua, that He was going to be fighting the battles for Him, so he changed his name to Jehovah. "his help". The name took any pride or ego that might develop because of the victories God would give Joshua. He taught Joshua that it won't be in his own natural strength that he would succeed, but that it would be only by God's strength and help that he would be able to be victorious. Now Joshua knew that God was his help in time of trouble, not his own might.

God startsC doing miracles for Joshua even early in his ministry. In Joshua, chapter 3 and 4 you see that God parted the waters of the Jordan. In Chapter 3:5 you see Joshua tells the people "tomorrow the Lord will do amazing things among you." He only gives glory to God and rested in His mighty power to fight for him. In verse 7, God tells Joshua, "I will exalt you in the eyes of all Israel." Why? Because he was humble and did what God commanded him to do. Remember (1 Peter 5:5-7) it says, "God opposes the proud, but gives grace to the humble. Humble yourselves therefore, under God's mighty hand, that he may lift you up in due time. Cast all your anxiety on Him because He cares for you." These are three awesome verses that show how we are to live. Verse 7 says "Cast all your anxiety on Him, because He cares for you." You see, He is there even when we might think He's not.

He wants us to release our battles and wars into His hands because then He can work it out for our good (Romans 8:28).

We all know the story of Joshua 6, "The Fall of Jericho," but what the story tells us is this, "we must learn to trust and rest in God's faithfulness." Joshua marched once around Jericho for six days, now you know that he must have been ridiculed by not only the people of Jericho, but probably his own people. They must have thought the boy has lost his mind. How are we going to defeat these people by marching around their city walls? Yet Joshua stood firm in his faith in God's faithfulness to deliver the people of Jericho into his hands.

You see the difference in what Biblical faith is and what is being taught today by many Bible teachers and others in the church. It's not a faith in your faith, but a faith in a person, Jesus Christ. On the seventh day, Joshua marched around the city seven times with the priest blowing the trumpet, and then the people shouted and the walls came tumbling down. Praise God! What an awesome mighty God we serve. At the end of chapter 6:27 it says, "so the Lord was with Joshua"....you see, it wasn't Joshua, but the Lord fighting for him.

In Chapter 10 we see that the sun stands still or the earth because the earth is the one that moves around the sun even though Joshua may have said it wrong, God knew what was in his heart. The Lord tells Joshua don't be afraid, I'll give them into your hands (Joshua 10:8).

Joshua not only defeats the five kings of the Amorites, who had joined forces to fight against him, but in verse 11 it says, "the Lord hurled large hailstones down from the sky and more of the Amorites died of the hailstones than from the swords of the Israelites." Verse 12 says "the Lord gave the Amorites to Israel."You see, it wasn't Joshua, but God who fought for him.

Then in verse 12 "Joshua says to the sun, stand still over Gibeon, O moon, over the Valley of Aijalon. So the sun stood still and the moon stopped, till the nation triumphed itself on its enemies." Verse 14, says "There has never been a day like it before or since." It was a day when the Lord listened to a man, surely the Lord was fighting for Israel. Everything that happened was God going before Israel fighting for them because of Joshua's faith in God's faithfulness.

It's an amazing thing that Joshua spoke to the sun and moon and they stood still, but you see in verse 14 even though Joshua spoke to the moon and sun to stop, it was God who did it. In the New Testament we read what Jesus said and is a great compliment to this story. He says "even if you have faith as small as a mustard seed, if you say to this mountain to be moved, it will move." (Matthew 21:21, Mark 11:22-23, Luke 17:5-6).

How do you win battles and war? It's not a how to formula or 12-step-process, but just learn to trust and rest in His ability to accomplish His will in your life, in His time.

BOOK EXCERPT: RISE UP IN TRIALS, TESTING AND SUFFERING

I'll open this chapter with a question I want you to answer honestly before you start reading this section. The question is this: Is God in everything, even evil and suffering?
You can answer this question by how you feel, or by faith. If you answer by feelings, they'll change, but by faith, you'll answer by what the word says.

The Lord allows trials, tests and sufferings, but He isn't the author or cause of evil and sufferings. Yes, God is in everything, but not the author of everything. Why do I say this? Because God isn't the author of the evil in this world (James 1:2-18). We must remember that sin and evil are real, (1 John 1:8, Romans 5:12-14, Hebrews 2:14-15) but also God never promised us freedom from pain and suffering. (Hebrews 2:18, 5:7-10, 1 Peter 4:12-19); it was exactly the opposite. God uses pain and suffering for His purposes. God takes evil and turns it around for our good (Romans 8:18-39, 2 Corinthians 12:1-10, James 1:3-4, 5:7-12). As children of God we have His promise of comfort and love (2 Corinthians 1:3-10; 2 Thessalonians 2:16-17).

Read the Gospels and the book of John, evil and suffering aren't experienced by any person as God's punishment for sins. (John 9:1-41 verse 2 and 3) Remember what I said, God uses pain and suffering for His purposes. This story illustrates just that. God has provided us a triumph, not us or what we do, but Jesus

Christ who has defeated death! Praise God! (1 Corinthians 15:35-58).

God gave each of us a free will; He didn't make us puppets that when He pushed the strings we move. No, He gave each of us a free choice so we could choose our own way, that's why Adam and Eve sinned. God wanted us to choose God. As you can see they disobeyed God and sinned and these were some of the consequences (James 1:2-18). God is a Holy, moral being and has structured the universe in such a way that natural consequences follow most of the good or evil choices we make.

He knows the future and allows it because of our free choice. Even though God may have our good in mind when we suffer, we often get angry, depressed, and confused at what's going on. Why? Because, let's face it, none of us wants to suffer or go through trials, but as long as we're living here on earth, we will experience suffering or trials, maybe not directly, but sometimes indirectly. This can occur by what may be happening to a friend, a spouse, or family member. However, the Lord said, I am faithful, and will strengthen and protect you from the evil one (2 Thessalonians 3:3).

He is faithful, and will not let you be tempted beyond what you can bare, but will provide a way out so that you can stand up under it. 1 Corinthians 10 is a great chapter because it gives us examples to learn from Israel's history and also about the believer's freedom in Christ. Verse 11 says, "Things happened as examples and were written as warnings to us." That is why when we are under trials, tests, or sufferings we should go look in the word and read about all the sufferings that happened to men like Job, Joseph, Paul, etc. and how they overcame, so that as examples we can learn from them.

The root of all this suffering is sin. When man fell in sin, forces were unleashed which have warped mankind and have an impact on the innocent as well as, the guilty. Every human life, which is involved in relationships with others is subject to pain, sufferings, and death. We are going to have to put on the garment of praise for the spirit of heaviness (Isaiah 61:3). Why do I say this? Because we are to rejoice in everything just like Paul and Silas did. They were singing and praising when they were in prison and you all know what happened, there was a great earthquake and the foundations of the prison were shaken and came loose, and the shackles were shaken and came loose. You can read the rest of the story in Acts 16:16-40.

Praise and worship breaks the spirit of depression and heaviness in our hearts and in many cases, we remain in this condition because we don't praise Him. We continue in the self-pity and we'll continue to stay there until we see that what we have is (Christ living in us) beyond a little pain here on earth.

I know you're saying, "It's easier said than done!" I know at times we will all feel alone, confused, and angry at what we feel is unfair to us. As children of God, we might feel like saying why us? Why do we have to go through all this pain and suffering, well you're not the only one going through suffering, (please try to put this in your heart when you suffer) hundreds, even thousands are going through the same sufferings all over the world.

You may not see results right away and think God is allowing this because of some secret sin. I'll tell you right now that's not it because there's no such thing as secret sin. God sees everything, and nothing is hidden from Him, nothing. (Job 34:21-23). If God was really going to punish us for our sins, we would be dead and in hell because that's what we deserve. Anything we have here on earth is just a privilege because we are just passing through; this isn't our home. We all deserve hell, for all have sinned and fallen short of the glory of God (Romans 3:23). But praise God, we now have eternal life because of Jesus Christ. What an awesome gift from God to us; sinners headed for hell, but He loved us so much that while we were still sinners He died for us. (Romans 5:8 and 6:23)

So I'll tell you something, it doesn't matter what you're going through, be it a death in the family, unemployment, marriage difficulties, or illness, etc. When you compare it to hell, you can smile! You can smile because we're not going to hell, we have passed from death unto life, yes, death unto life! Praise God and rejoice in this because we have won!

We must have the joy of the Lord in our lives, or else there's a problem. We have something that the whole world is looking for. We have the joy and peace of God that surpasses all understanding (Philippians 4:6-7).

If Moses, Paul, Joseph, Jesus had to go through suffering, what makes us so special that we shouldn't have to. Paul said he rejoiced in sufferings (2 Corinthians 6:3-13, 2 Cor. 7:2-16, 2 Cor. 12:10, Acts 2, 28).

One of the biggest impacts in my life has been 2 Corinthians Chapter 11:16-33 and 2 Corinthians 12:1-10 because the Lord taught me through Paul's writings that sometimes we're not healed from physical infirmities, but He will use them for His glory. These are the times when we learn to trust and rest in Him during times of sufferings. Paul says something in 2 Cor. 11:30 that changed my way of thinking and living, "If I boast, I'll boast of things that show my weakness."

When I was 10 years old, I developed Rheumatism or Rheumatoid Arthritis. It causes weakness in your bones, your joints to become brittle and creates a situation where both bones and joints get inflamed and easily injured. I suffered with pain in my body 24 hours a day, 7 days a week, and 365 days a year.

When I was younger I would cry myself to sleep almost every night because not only did I have Rheumatism, but I suffered from migraine headaches and ear aches as well. Of course, they can prescribe pain medicine and other medications, but it never really eliminates all the pain. I became a Christian around the time I developed all these infirmities. I was given doctor's notes to skip gym class which always made me feel alone and left out and it was because of this I became shy around people.

Many of the kids would make fun of me and say I was a weakling, lazy or faking it. In 5th grade I had a gym teacher that knew how much I loved sports and how I wanted to play. He allowed me to play softball, whiffle ball, and all the other games the kids were playing, though he wasn't supposed to because of the notes from doctor and Mom. He knew that I wanted to take part with the class. I got some bruises along the way, but I loved it because I was now making friends in elementary school and the other kids were no longer laughing at me.

As I entered middle school and high school, I was not a popular student and mostly kept to myself except for a few select friends. I never developed into the baseball star that I longed to become, but I became an avid baseball fan and learned all the stats in sports, especially baseball. While I was on the St. Peter's Lutheran Church Softball team, I kept all the team stats on computer. I even made it to the All-Star team once with a .346 average, but never played in the All-Star Game.

Through it all, God has given me the strength to do all these things, even today. I praise God every day for giving me supernatural strength to do things that I know I wouldn't be able to do in my own strength. For many years I thought my sickness was due to something wrong I must have done and maybe I didn't have enough faith to be healed. I would pray the prayer Paul prayed to the Lord in 2 Corinthians 12:8-9, "take it away," but each time I would hear "My grace is sufficient for you, for my power is made perfect in weakness," verse 10,"for when I'm weak He is strong."

It has taken me many years to see just how my weaknesses have blessed my life and others. I know through my testimony I am able to minister to people who may be going through the same sufferings (2 Corinthians 4:8). That's one of the reasons God may allow trials, tests, or sufferings in our lives. Also, I know if I would have been completely healed of everything, I would have become consumed with the other things I wanted to do and would have probably become conceited and unable to witness to others.

I most certainly would not be here today writing this and serving as an assistant pastor of a church. Yes, the Lord did call me to the ministry, as He showed me many years ago preaching in a church, but I never would have believed it because of my shyness, but I knew it would happen because the vision the Lord had given me.

Yes we suffer in this life. Yes, the Lord provided an example for me through the Apostle Paul's sufferings. Yes, He still can heal and does still heal today, as He has done for me in other areas. He is the one who decides it, and wills it according to His plan. No matter what is being taught in the church today on how you can make God heal you, or decree it into existence; you have no power to decree something into existence. You're not God, you have to pray according to His will because He's the one who's in control, not you (Proverbs 16:1-4; 9; Proverbs 20:18, 24; Proverbs 21:2; 30-31).

If you can decree it into existence, why are there still sick people, and even Christians that profess to be able to decree things into existence that still die? Why? Because the Lord has your days already numbered, and no matter what, when your day comes to die, you're going to die no matter what you say. (Job 14:5-12, Isaiah 43:1). They may even say, they are still sick because they had no faith, or died because of no faith. By saying that they just called themselves a liar.

Why? Because if they can decree something into existence, then even though the person had no faith, they still would be healed because they decreed it! That means that decreeing something doesn't work, it's a way of controlling people, so they don't question their unbiblical teachings! Brethren, Jesus Himself suffered. He had to go through such an intense suffering that it says He cried tears of blood even before the physical suffering had begun. (Luke 22:44). If our King of Kings had to go through suffering beyond human comprehension, then why should we be exempt from suffering? Jesus suffered so we could live (1 Peter 3:8-22; 1 Peter 4:12-19).

Jesus showed us examples on how to pray. He said not my will, but the will of the father be done. What an awesome word for us. What more of an example can we get? If He himself said this, how much more should we pray (Matt. 26:39; Mark 14:36; Luke 22:42; John 15, 17).

Another thing we must learn is "If our faith depends upon seeing a miracle every time we suffer, it's not faith at all, it's just inner doubt looking for proof from God that He's there" (2 Corinthians 1:4). We must also remember that the devil is prince of the power of the air (Job 1 & 2; 1 Peter 5:8), so he will try anything to get you to question God's providence, and to doubt God's faithfulness (2 Thessalonians 3:3).

Why do righteous people suffer? Maybe because they are righteous! It's a simple answer, but sometimes difficult to comprehend. We must remember that Satan hates the children of God which are made righteous because of Christ's death and resurrection and because of His free gift of grace.

God may allow Satan to bring calamities, temptation, or tests to His people similar as He did with Job. Even Jesus was tempted and tested in the desert (John 1, 2; Matthew 4:1-11; Mark 1: 9-13; Luke 4: 1-13). Why? Well in Jesus' situation, it was different because it was His mission to experience everything we do. One difference is that He didn't sin by giving in to temptation, (Luke 4:1-13) He was the perfect, holy-sacrifice; a man, yet fully God, without sin or blemish. For us it may be because many times we have to be reminded to trust in Him, in any situation good or bad.

Many times we rejoice only when things are going well for us, but when something comes along that disrupts our daily lives, we get on the offense and complain, mumble, or blame God. We all do it, and that is why it may be allowed, to bring about perseverance and maturity (James 1:2-18, Rom. 5). Even if you suffer, you are blessed (1 Peter 3:14). Be assured that God will bring you out at the right time. The Bible says, "He'll rescue Godly men from trials." (2 Peter 2:9). He protected Noah, a preacher of righteousness and seven others and He rescued Lot from Sodom and Gomorrah. (2 Peter 2:5-8).

We too must have faith in any circumstance because no matter what happens to us, if we live or die, we have a building from God, an eternal house in heaven, not built by human hands. Meanwhile we groan, longing to be clothed with our heavenly dwelling because when we are clothed we will not be found naked.

While we are in this tent, we groan and are burdened because we do not wish to be unclothed, but to be clothed with our heavenly dwelling so that what is mortal may be swallowed up by life.

Now, it is God who has made us for this very purpose and has given us the spirit as a deposit, guaranteeing what is to come. Therefore we are always confident and know that as long as we are at home in the body we are away from the Lord. We live by faith, not by sight. We are confident, I say, and would prefer to be away from the body and at home with the Lord. So we make it our goal to please Him whether we are at home in the body or away from it. (2 Corinthians 5:1-9).

Why do we as blood-bought children of God, made righteous in God's eyes by His grace, still suffer? Why do trials still come our way and why are our hearts still tested? These are questions that have been asked for centuries? I want you to ponder on this answer from God's mouth because He answers us with a question: If you don't understand what is, How are you going to understand what ought to be? (Proverbs 20:24).

For my thoughts aren't your thoughts and never are your ways my ways declares the Lord, "As the heavens are higher than the earth, so are my ways higher than your ways and my thoughts than your thoughts. So is My word that goes out from my mouth, will not return to me empty, but will accomplish what I desire and achieve the purposes from which I sent it." (Isaiah 55:8-9, 11). Mostly all the people God used in the Bible, went through rejection, tests, sufferings and wilderness experiences. These experiences not only strengthen them, but build them up to be able to overcome the sufferings, and glory in what they went through.

Why? Because they knew that what they were going through was going to lift up God in the eyes of the people they would minister to.

Here are some examples of Biblical characters from their beginnings and rejection, to places of leadership (Read Proverbs 19): Rejections and Wilderness Experiences
:
Paul, 14 years of obscurity = Apostle.
Joseph, 13 years in Prison = Throne in Egypt
Moses, 40 years in Wilderness = Deliverer, Prophet
Joshua, 40 years in Wilderness = Captain and Chief Shepherd of Israel
Jesus, 3 1/2 years of Rejection = King of Kings, Lord of Lords

You can see that God didn't give Joshua, Moses, Joseph and Paul the full extent of their ministry all at once. It was progressive;

He revealed it to them gradually. God didn't reveal everything at once because they might have destroyed both their life and their ministry by trying to help God fulfill it.

BOOK EXCERPT: SERVING GOD
WITH GRACE AND TRUTH

Why are you serving God? Is it for the things that He will bless you with or because of Him?

We all need to be really honest about this because we need to serve our God with grace and truth and not with expectations of glory for us. Jesus did just the opposite of what many do today, Jesus had glory before the world began and yet He left his glory because He heard our cries and came to serve us (John 17:3-5, 22, Col. 1:15-23; Heb. 2:5-18).

We are to serve all who come to us for help and guidance. We are to accept all whose faith is weak, without passing judgment on disputable matters. We aren't supposed to look down on anyone who's struggling in whatever situation it might be because God has accepted Him through Christ (Romans. 14:1-3). We are to serve God the same way Christ Jesus did, wholeheartedly and without visions of glory and fame.

For the Kingdom of God isn't a matter of eating and drinking, but of righteousness, peace, and joy in the Holy spirit, because anyone who serves Christ in this way is pleasing to God and approved by men (Rom. 14:17-18). We are to serve with joy and peace in our hearts because we are children of the living God and because of what He has done for us. When we serve Him this way and not for our benefits or good, God will be pleased because it's from the heart.

We are to give to those that are in need in whatever way possible, be it with financial aid or with prayer or with physical help to build them up, no matter the cost to us. For Christ didn't please himself but, as it is written: "The insults of those who insult you have fallen on me." For what was written in the past was written to teach us so that through endurance and encouragement of the scriptures we might have hope (Rom. 15:1-4). Verse 3, is a powerful verse, it tells us Christ took our insults or in other words our trials and temptations on Himself so we wouldn't have to bare them on our own. This verse reminds us not to give up and to go to Him who brings peace in and through the storms.

May the God who gives endurance and encouragement give you the spirit of unity among yourselves, (the body of Christ) as you follow Christ Jesus, so that with one heart and mouth you may glorify the God and Father of our Lord Jesus Christ. Accept one another then, just as Christ accepted you in order to bring praise to God (Romans 15:5-7).

Christ never intended us to have so many denominations that cause quarrels amongst each other due to man-made rules which leaders of the movement, may or may have not created. Religions, rules, and regulations from the many different denominations in the body of Christ are not what Christ gave to us.

Religion was what Christ came to speak against because He was looking for people who would love Him because of what He did. Christianity isn't about religion or being religious, but about a relationship with Christ. The word religion in the Greek, meant a return to bondage, that is exactly what all the religious systems of our world bring, bondage to a set of rules of "Do's" and "Don't" with no real relationship with Christ who came to set us free from the law and it's requirements.(Heb. 9 and 10, I Cor. 3 and 4).

Paul wrote in Romans 15:17-19, "Therefore I glory in Christ Jesus in my service to God. I will not venture to speak of anything except what Christ has accomplished through me in leading the gentiles to obey God by what I have said and done, by the power of signs and miracles, through the power of the Spirit." He continued, "Let us glory in what Christ has done through us," and nothing else, that's the way we are to serve!

If we as Christians can get along and proclaim the Gospel of Christ, we could really impact society with the true gospel, not religious laws, but with the transforming power of the grace of God through Christ's blood that has given us life eternally (Romans 10).

We must love God completely and without reservation. In the old testament in Deuteronomy 4:29, it says, "But if from there you seek the Lord your God, you will find Him if you look for Him with all your heart and with all your soul." In the New Testament it goes even further to proclaim the devotion we should have to God, in Mark 12:30, it says, "And you shall love your God with all your heart, and with all your soul, and with all your mind, and with all your strength." That is more powerful than what the Old Testament says.

We are to love God with our whole being. Loving God involves not only our emotions, but our intellect and our will. It involves our whole personality which doesn't mean we're puppets on a string. Many think you rely on God because you're weak or you don't know the power you have in and of yourself. They tell us, don't you know that we are gods, just like the God you claim is the real one.

Unfortunately, I have heard many people say these things even some who claim to be Christians, but these statements demonstrate they don't really know God. If they did they would understand the nature of God and His deeds and see we're not gods or little gods because He's in control! If we are gods or little gods we would be able to control world peace, stop hunger, death, and disease on this place we call earth, but we can't, so we are not gods!

The Bible (Deuteronomy 4:32-33) speaks about the weak and the strong. Yes, there may be some that are physically or spiritually stronger in our world, but the Bible doesn't speak about weakness in the same light as the world sees it. The world sees weakness as a liability, but the Bible speaks of it as strength.

When we are at the weakest in all the sense of the word, be it emotionally, physically or intellectually, we are strongest in our relationship with God, knowing that we in our ourselves can do nothing to get us out of our trouble (John 15:5). When we allow God to take control He always rescues us out of the storm and our sin, even when we don't understand what is happening.

The Bible tells us that when we're in distress and troubled, even if we try to walk away from the Lord, God will always be with us and you will come back to him because of His promises and mercy towards you. You will realize that apart from Him life is meaningless, even with great material possessions. For you will discover that the Lord is a merciful God, He will never abandon or destroy you or forget you (Deuteronomy 4:30-31).

We are to take the scriptures to heart, for they are life and peace to us. We are all given a choice in this life, to either choose life or death, blessings or curses. If we truly understand what choosing life means then we will come to know the God of Abraham, Isaac, and Jacob; the one who gave us His son Jesus Christ as an example on how we are to live, if we accept and receive Him as Lord of all.

Deuteronomy 30:20 says, "And that you may love the Lord your God, listen to his voice, and hold fast to Him; for the Lord is your life and He will give you many years in the land he swore to give to your fathers, Abraham, Isaac, Jacob." In later chapters, I'll discuss the covenant God had with Abraham. Let us remember always, the Lord is our life, He's the one who truly gives you purpose in life and it will last through all eternity.

We must be strong and courageous, not of ourselves, but through the almighty God living in us. He will give us that strength and boldness, believe me when I say this for I myself am timid and fearful, but through Christ He has and is still giving me courage and boldness in Christ. Be strong and courageous, don't be afraid or terrified because of them for the Lord God goes with you. He will never leave you or forsake you (Deuteronomy 31:6). If God goes with us who can stand against us, nothing in all creation can separate us from the love of God in Christ Jesus (Romans 8:32, 35-39).

The reason we as Christians are able to serve God in grace and truth is because He first loved us. That same unconditional love caused Him to send His only son to die for us. That causes us to want to know Him more, and when that happens we grow in the wisdom and knowledge of Jesus Christ which surpasses knowledge (Ephesians 3:19).

We love Him because He first loved us, and the more we discover the pure love God gave freely, we will better serve Him with grace (unmerited favor) and truth (not false, faithful, loyal, sure). The more we learn of God the more our hearts will respond in love for Him and also for our fellow man. In Christ we have the security that we have longed for all our lives.

God loved us because He chooses to love us, it was free and undeserved. That causes us to serve the Lord with all our strength, in whatever we do. He's our source of joy in the world and the joy He gives will never fade.

Ephesians 6:6-7 says, "Doing the will of God from your heart, serve wholeheartedly, as if you were serving the Lord, not man." We are to serve everyone as if it were God himself that we were helping. Why? Because many times we will help people that will never say thank you to us or even care to, but that must not stop us from losing heart because we are doing it unto God for his glory.

With sincerity of heart and perseverance for the Lord, whatever you do, work at it with all your heart, as working for the Lord, not for men (Colossians 3:22-24). No one should seek his own good, but the good of others (1 Corinthians 10:24), we are not like the world, for we are to put others before ourselves for their good.

We are to proclaim good news to all we can, no matter what the cost to us, for we are eternally secure in Christ. Whoever serves me must follow me and where I am, my servant also will be. My father will honor the one who serves me. A voice came from heaven, you are gloried and Jesus said the voice was for your benefit, not mine (John 12:26-28, 30). For whoever wants to be first, must become a servant, just as the Son of Man didn't come to be served, but to serve, and to give His life as a ransom for many (Matthew 20:27-28).

We are to serve first and not think about our position or title in the church or out of the church. Many in the church only think of position and power to control people to do their bidding. That is unbiblical, for if Jesus Christ came not to be served, but to serve us, then if we are leaders, pastors or elders, we must be servants to the body of Christ. That is what a leader is called to do, to serve to the best of their ability for the good of the people they are serving.

Paul wrote in 2 Corinthians 1:8-9, "We were under great pressure, far beyond our ability to endure, so that we despaired even of life, indeed in our hearts we felt the sentence of death. But this happened that we might not rely on ourselves, but on God, who raises the Dead." Serving God with grace and truth demonstrates it's out of our hands and that we have to rely on God 100% to lead us to victory. What is grace? "Power beyond our own ability."

I want to write what I believe the Lord told me concerning this issue of serving, you can take it as prophecy or as a confirmation or whatever way you want, but I'm going to write it just as the Lord gave it to me to write:

"I've heard the cries from the foundations of the world and I came to serve you, so that because of my love, you would serve Me. All through the ages I've heard the cries of my people and even in death I've made their bedside a cathedral of faith and love for serving Me. Not because they had to, but because they choose to serve Me. I'm never looking for people who have to, but for whosoever will.

Make your hearts an open door to reach those who are hurt, depressed and lost, give my joy to them, just as you have received. Put your hands around the lonely so that their broken hearts can mend, because what you have received is full of life and love. That same life must spring forth from your heart, soul, mind, and strength, so that you can also give that same life to others.

Hear the cries around you and serve because of the grace that you have also received. My grace is sufficient, because it's power beyond your own ability. You are to rejoice in the grace of God, not ponder it. In the name of Jesus you have everything you need."

BOOK EXCERPT: RAGING STORMS AND WAR! RISE AND PREPARE TO OVERCOME THE STORMS

Some of the storms in our lives are sent, allowed or created. There are two kinds of storms:

Correctional Storms: Those that are sent to correct our ways.
Perfectional Storms: These are sent to mature us. Why? Because God is equipping us to overcome the storms that come our way and use them to minister to others going through similar storms. When storms come our way we usually forget past spiritual experiences which served to get us through the storms to come. That's why it's good to keep a journal on the things that God does in our

lives, so in bad times you can go back and see that God works everything for good (Romans 8:18-39). This will help you to keep your mind on Christ and know that the Jesus that brought you through that past problem is the same Jesus now in this problem.

He doesn't change, He's always there (Hebrews 13:8). We just have to realize, He's in control and keep our eyes on Him. (Matthew 6:33; Matthew 3:23). It's in the midst of the storm that we need to be reminded of what God has done for us, and is continuing to do. The storms may be different, but God isn't, He's the same yesterday, today and forever. (Hebrews 13:8).
When the storms come, Christ is aware! Don't think He's on vacation. Christ knows what you're feeling; put your mind on this. (Roman 15).

Just because you might not feel his presence does not mean He's not there. We should know not to go by feelings anyway because feelings always change, but God doesn't (Hebrew 13:8). If we know that He's there, then we have an assurance that everything is going to be alright, no matter what comes or happens that's the way we are to live – not scared or worried about our salvation throughout life's storms. We've already won the war; we're on the winning side. Jesus already defeated the sting of death; let's learn to rest in it (Romans 6 and 8; Ephesians 2; Hebrews 10; 2 Timothy 1:7-10; 1 Corinthians 15:35-58.) Light and darkness don't blind God's eyes to what is going on in our lives, light and darkness are the same to Him, He created both and He was in control of both (Genesis 1).

Light and darkness have no effect on God; He can see though time itself, so rest in his sufficiency. Learn to take your eyes off yourself and your problem and look to Him and see what He has done for you and will continue to do. Learn to do this and Christ will do the rest. The Bible says "The Battle belongs to the Lord." (Deuteronomy 20:4; 1 Chronicles 5:20, 22). That's it 100%, learn to rest in this, He is in control and will make a way out at the right time. We might not care to hear this in our storms, but we need to rely on His promises that He is there for us in every situation.

Christ also meets us in every storm. Register this in your heart and mind and leave it there forever. Know this, Christ does not go on vacation and stops hearing you or seeing the problems you're facing. Know that every inch of the universe and everything that is created is in His presence every hour of every day. So He does see us in every situation, so don't ever think that He's not there when you need Him because He is! (1 Chronicles 10:13)

Refer to the example in the Gospels when the storm came while the disciples and Jesus were in the boat. He waited until the disciples were worn out and scared to stop the storms. Does it mean that Jesus didn't care because He left them on their own? Jesus allowed this because they weren't looking to Him in the storm.

They were focusing on themselves and what they could do to get themselves out of the storm. Then they got scared and knew they couldn't override the storm so they went to get Jesus up from His sleep. You see that is an example of what we also do with Jesus when we have a problem; we do exactly the same thing. We usually try to overcome our storms on our own and we fall or can't handle them, so then we run to Christ for help; having no faith in his sufficiency to complete the work in us. (Mark 4:35-41; Luke 8:22-25; John 6:16-24).

If you're going through a storm right now and you're saying, "God, where are you? Why don't you do something? What are you waiting for?" I want to ask you this: Isn't it wonderful that God doesn't answer?

I'm sure you're probably thinking it's not wonderful when we don't hear an answer, but know that God is there. You may not see Him or hear Him, but He's there. You know what He does? He listens and doesn't become angry, upset or doesn't condemn or threaten us due to unbelief in His sufficiency. He just listens to us quietly while we complain and mumble because He doesn't meet our schedule and time clock. Why does it seem to us that He waits too long? He doesn't meet our schedule and time clock?

First of all, His ways and time are not like ours. (Isaiah 55:8) He's always in the process of teaching us. When we are weak is when we usually are our strongest in our dependency on Him; knowing that without Him we are nothing (John 15:5). Jesus knows when to rescue us from out of our storms at just the right time.

Sometimes when we're in the midst of the storm, Jesus is right there and we don't see Him. Why? Because we expect Him to do things in either black or white. Let me give you an example: We need a car to get to work and God supplies the car, but the car breaks down. You get upset because you can't get to work now, but a friend happens to come by in their car and takes you to work. You might be upset because of your car, but didn't God supply the car in your friend when they took you to work.

Think about it. Your car was probably experiencing issues long before that time; God already knowing this sent a friend to take you to work. Praise God! Isn't God awesome, He knows what we don't know and we probably would not understand even if we did know. As it says in Proverbs 20:24, "A man's steps are directed by the Lord, how then can anyone understand his own way?"

But many times what we do is this: we don't expect God to come a certain way, and when He doesn't, we get discouraged. Many times we try to put God in a box, and if He doesn't fit in our box we start thinking things like, where are you God? Why don't you answer me? Many times the solution may be right in front of us. In all of our storms God always gives us encouragement or a way out. God doesn't just let us waste away even though it may appear that way. Godly encouragement could come to us in many ways, it could come from a friend, through His word or through prayer.

If storms come our way and into our lives, then God has allowed it for a purpose even if we don't see it always or understand it at the moment we're going through it. God never does anything just to do it. He always has purpose and direction in whatever is happening to us or around us (Isaiah 55:11). God will always make things clear to us and we don't have to be running around, confused and fearful of the unexpected. You may think, 'Why?' Because God doesn't give us a spirit of fear, but of a sound mind (2 Timothy 1:7).

Many times we have to hit rock bottom to finally see that we in and of ourselves can do nothing to stop the circumstances that come our way. Only then, do most of us run to Christ with our storms, so He can take control of them. The storms in this life may in many instances be sent or allowed to lead us from the bondage of self-worship. I'm talking about, not knowing the sufficiency of Christ's work on the cross.

Remember this statement and focus on "work" because the work that Christ (and only Christ, not us) did on the cross is meant to free us from bondage to the law and its requirements (Gal. 5). We aren't' supposed to work anymore to attain salvation or to attain a better standing before God. What usually happens is that we try to work our salvation and it becomes just that, "our" salvation.

The grace of God is truly a free gift without measure given to us who believe in Him as the only way of salvation given to man, so that no man can boast. Only Christ is given the glory, no one else is given to us to be saved, but only Christ made the way to life (Ephesians 2:8-10; 1 Tim. 2:5; Heb. 2). Many times we forget that the Lord Jesus Christ didn't say, "I have come that they may have life, if they work out their salvation. And the grace of God isn't a free gift, so that many may boast. No, the Lord Jesus Christ came to give His life for us that He might live His life through us for us not rely on ourselves or in our works. It's only through His life that we have life!

Trying to work out your salvation will only cause frustration, depression and bondage, why? Because you'll be trying to live up to a standard that your incapable of living up to because you would have to be 100% perfect and sinless which we are not! You can't be Jesus because once you were born you were disqualified; we are all born with a sin nature, we have all fallen short of the glory of God for all have sinned (Rom. 3:9-29). We must put aside our attempt to be little Jesus' because we will only frustrate ourselves trying to reach it, you'll end up in a state of spiritual burnout.

We are now living in a new covenant of grace, but the law isn't evil, it's Holy, given from God to the nation of Israel through Moses. Moses was one of the greatest prophets to walk the earth, but man couldn't live up to the holy requirements of the law because if you broke one commandment you were guilty of breaking them all. So God chose a greater way to give us life and communion with Him. He gave Abram (whose name later would be changed to Abraham) the Gospel of faith which was grace given to him by God.

Yes, I'll say it again, yes, God gave Abraham the Gospel of grace even though it was many years before Christ would come to fulfill that Gospel of faith (Grace). Amazingly, it has been in the scriptures all through the ages, but many have not seen it, if you are one of those who think God changed His plans on how He was going to save us, allow me to speak to you about how it was always grace even in the Old Testament.

BOOK EXCERPT: SHOUT AND FIGHT

I'm writing this book so that many may come to a full understanding of our true identity in Christ and to give encouragement to those that are experiencing temptations and sufferings in their lives.

What do I have to shout and fight about? What we have in the body of Christ should be shouted from the rooftops! Christ has given us life, freedom and a peace that surpasses anything in our world. Yet many in the body of Christ live like they have no freedom and peace. Why? Because they don't know the sufficiency of Christ's finished work on the cross. Many may say, what are you talking about? I know what Christ did for me at the cross. That's true of all who have accepted Christ as their personal Savior, but they haven't yet learned the full impact of what His life and sacrifice were all about. God's grace was given to give life and freedom in our Christian walk, yet many live in a life of rules and regulations, do's and don'ts and are burdened with weights that no man should carry.

Many of us live trying to obtain a holy and righteous status before God with our good works, but that's just the opposite of what Christ taught us from the scriptures. It's not wrong to want to live a life worthy of the calling God has given you, but Christ came to die for our sins so that through His death and resurrection we might have a righteous standing before God (Romans 3:21-24). When we learn to understand that we no longer are seen by God as unholy, unrighteous people, but as His righteous children justified by His blood (Romans 5:1-11; Hebrew 9) we then can be set free from the law and it's requirements. Christ said if I set you free you will be free indeed (John 8:32-36).

In Paul's writings you see how Paul had to come against those who were trying to put the new believers back into the law and its yoke of slavery on them again after receiving the truth of God's Grace. (Galatians 3).

We have to understand that God isn't out to get us, He gave His son so that we would have life and have it more abundantly (John 10:10). We need to understand that we have total forgiveness in Christ. Christ died for us while we were yet sinners, before we were even born. I can't lose that same forgiveness when I fall or mess up because I can't lose what was established before I was born. I'm not saying or giving you a license to sin, but just the opposite; knowing totally that because of His love and mercy we are compelled to serve Him with all of our hearts. Romans 6 speaks about this same issue and Paul is very strong in His response to our question, should we then take this as license to sin? But just as Paul said, "by no means, because we died to sin, and we can no longer live in it."

We are to live 100% under the grace of God and that means to look 100% to Christ for all our needs because apart from Christ we can do nothing (John 15:5). I know many, will disagree with me on this issue, but I see it as a great learning experience to be able to stand on what I believe. The scriptures are teaching me to be able to love any who disagree.

I will continue to shout the message of total forgiveness in Christ because I believe it's the only message that will free the body of Christ of a works and religious mentality. If we are free from that we can impact our city, society, and the world without religious restriction. It's not about being religious or a religion, but about a person, Jesus Christ our Savior and a personal relationship with Him. Many of us try to bring people into our church or religion instead of to Christ. Christ is the one, who has to do the work in their lives, don't be so afraid of giving everything to Christ so that He can work it out for his glory.

We always try to do things on our own and they end up being a problem for us and also for others.

Let's look at some examples in the Old Testament about how we should rely on God 100%. The account begins in 2 Samuel

11, "King David sends his army out to war, but doesn't go himself, he stays in Jerusalem. David then takes a walk on the roof of the palace and sees Bathsheba bathing and commits sin." David did something on his own that he thought would work itself out, after all he was the King of the great nation of Israel, he was a military hero, the slayer of the giant Goliath, surely he could have or do as he pleased and it would work itself out. But the actions he took were of his own wisdom and desires. God would forgive him and restore him, but if he had sought out Gods counsel none of these sufferings would have happened. We all must reap what we sow, even though we're totally secure and forgiven in Christ. If we reap to the flesh, we will reap death. If we sow to the Spirit, we will reap life (Galatians 6:7-11).

King David went from being lazy to lusting with the eyes and then committing adultery to finally committing murder. Many may say, as long as you don't hurt anyone else, go ahead and do it if you want, just remember don't hurt anybody else. King David thought he wasn't hurting anyone at first.

He said, I'll stay home from the war. Yet, we will never know how many men he could have been spared had he gone to war with his men, as was expected of him. Then he calls for Bathsheba and sleeps with her and thought no one will be the wiser, nobody will know, her husband's off to war, who'll know. However, Bathsheba gets pregnant. David sends for Uriah, Bathsheba's husband and sends him home so he could sleep with his wife and then she could say the baby was Uriah's.

But Uriah was an honest, obedient soldier and didn't want to go home while the war was still going on and his men were in the battlefield. King David then devices a plan to kill Uriah, no one is going to get hurt, but he becomes a murderer to cover up his evil deed. Read 2 Samuel, 12-19 to see all the events that follow this one decision that David made.

I'll summarize the events: David has a son from Bathsheba, but the baby dies, then his son Amnon rapes his sister and then Absalom kills Amnon his brother for raping his sister. David then allows Absalom to flee and to then come back, but Absalom conspires to over throw David his father and take over the kingdom by force. In the battle not only does Absalom his son die, but over 20,000 men.

What happened to David's children? Through all his children's rebellion and disobedience, David failed to discipline his children. They deserved severe punishment accordingly to the law, but David let them off with hardly a word. Perhaps his own guilt, over what he had done in the past, affected his sense of discipline toward his children. What's the point of this account? That whenever we do anything of ourselves and think we won't hurt anyone else think again because the consequences can be far worst then you think. Yes, we're secure and totally forgiven, but we reap what we sow on this earth. If you steal and are caught you'll go to jail; those are the governmental laws of this country.

King David did what many of us do today, we try in our own wisdom to overcome our problems and we suffer the consequences. David didn't rely on God to lead him when he made his decision to stay home that day and three of his sons died and over 20,000 men.

That's why we are to rely 100% on Christ's finished work on the cross and Him doing the work, in and through us because without him we are nothing (John 15:5). David was forgiven, but the consequences of what he did and the lives it affected would be with him all the days of his life (Romans 5:12-21).

Jesus says in John 6:29, "The work of the father is this, believe in the one He has sent." There are works in the ministry we do, but not because it's part of salvation, but because of salvation. It should be a privilege and a joy to help people and to pray for them because you want people to experience the same joy and peace we have. That's the reason that we should be doing works or service in the body. As Jesus said, "I have come that they may have life and have it to the fullest (John 10:10), also he said in (Luke 4:18-19), "I have come to preach good news to the poor, to proclaim freedom for the prisoners, and recovery of sight to the blind, to release the oppressed, to proclaim the year of the Lord's favor."

We aren't saved by works or the service we do, but part of being a believer is doing service in the body of Christ to benefit others for the cause of Christ. Yes, Paul wrote, inspired by the Holy Spirit for it is by grace you have been saved. Through faith and this not from yourselves, it's the gift of God not by works, so that no one can boast, but many of us forget the next verse and no it's not a contradiction. Let's read this next verse, "For we are God's workmanship, created in Christ Jesus to do good works, which God prepared in advance for us to do (Ephesians 2:8-10).

Paul makes it clear, good works do nothing to help us obtain favor of salvation from God, but as we come to experience God's love and favor towards us, good works or service will follow because of that love which he has shown us. If you're doing works for any other reason, be it for better standing, for your church or for your own self-esteem, that's not going to give you peace or bring rest because there will always be something more to do. You will live your life with no assurance of your own salvation, let alone other's that you may have spoken to.

If we believe in Christ and believe we are born again by his shed blood on the cross we must understand what happened at the cross and how through that one sacrifice, we are set free for all eternity. We are to rest in that grace that God provided through Christ for us. Then all other things will follow (Matthew 6:33). The scriptures say we are sealed with the Holy Spirit and that it's

(Salvation) kept in heaven for us and it will never perish, spoil or fade, who through faith are shielded by God's power (1 Peter 1:3-5).

What do we as children of the Light fight about? It's not a physical fight but a spiritual fight. We fight in prayer when we pray for others to know Christ and for them to be delivered from darkness. Many may wonder who we are really fighting against. Are we fighting those who don't believe in Christ? The atheist, the agnostic or the cults; some may even say, how about those who say they believe in Christ, like some new agers or skinheads? Shouldn't we fight physical battles to stop these teachings/people in the name of Christ?

That exactly is what we feel like doing sometimes, but that isn't the way Christ taught us. Some may say, as Christians, are we supposed to let the liberals run this nation to the ground and allow the abortions to continue, the homosexual agenda and the Satanist go on without opposition.

No, we are called to oppose everything that God calls evil, but yet we must be careful how we make our stand. Is it in (Galatians 4:18) anger and hatred? This will only lead to violence and death. I've seen many demonstrations against one thing or another that so called "Christians" were involved in, and it makes you wonder what happened to Christ's words, "love your neighbors as yourselves." Some have become so enthralled in "their" stand that it has put them in bondage to the cause and they've abandoned their convictions. Once they approached these issues with purity of heart, but now their actions grieve the Spirit of God.

What do I mean when I say this? Well it's simple: Christ hasn't called us to wound and kill everyone who disagrees with us or to kill the so called wicked because you're right. I know many are fed up with American society and how we are living in this nation. Some feel they need to do something now because we're heading toward anarchy. I know that's what many are saying and thinking, but we are called to fight battles and wars on our knees because the battle is the Lord's (1 Chronicles 5:22; Deuteronomy 20:4; 1 Samuel 18:17).

Do you recall David's cry after he had defeated Goliath. He said, "All those gathered here will know that it is not by sword or spear that the Lord saves; for the battle is the Lord's and he will give all of you into our hands (1 Samuel 17:47). What a mighty prophetic stanza from David's mouth to us today as we fight the forces of darkness in the world today.

David, even though he had just defeated Goliath in a physical battle, says, "It's not by sword or spear, but by His spirit leading us and giving us the victory." We as Christians must learn to leave the sword buried once and for all and learn from David's mighty stanza. God will give them into our hands by his transforming power and might, not by the force of our hands. That's why I mentioned that we must understand the power of the cross because when we understand that, we can rest in the midst of the storms and have the peace that surpasses understanding, that's what will engulf us in His promises.

Remember that Christ said, "If we live by the sword, we will die by it" (Matt. 26:52). We aren't supposed to give wrath a place in our hearts. What type of witness are we giving the unbelievers if that's our response. What sort of Godly love are we to offer if it's brought in blood?

So who are we really fighting against? The word of God tells us in Ephesians 6:12, "For our struggle is not against flesh and blood, but against the rulers, against the authorities, against the powers of this dark world and against the spiritual forces of evil in the heavenly realms." So, "Put on the full armor of God, so that when the day of evil comes, you may be able to stand your ground." We must learn to fight on our knees in prayer; many

Christians including myself have failed to do so and are now learning, for God to work in all things, we must place it in God's hand and He will lead and guide us! (Proverbs 20:24).

If you don't have a peace about what Christ has totally done for you on the cross, you will never have the full armor of God. We have to begin to put God's word in our hearts and more importantly believe it. This is not dependent on our desires or effort, but God's mercy (Rom. 9:16). If we can get this in our hearts, we will have a peace that will lead us to totally depend on God, and then the armor will overcome because we are looking to Him, one hundred percent, to fight our battles.

Law and grace do not mix, they will only cause us to fear that we may have some secret sin or something unpleasing to God. So your battles will always reflect this thinking and it will bring defeat sooner or later. Some may say, "What do you mean? There are no secret sins in people's lives?"

I, myself was a little troubled by this and the Lord led me to read Hebrews 4:13-14, which says, "Nothing in all creation is hidden from God's sight. Everything is uncovered and laid bare before the eyes of Him to whom we must give account." So there isn't such a thing as secret sin because God sees everything and nothing is hidden from Him. That is a term that is used often to keep people in bondage to the rules and regulations of others. The bondage of sin was destroyed at the cross (Read Romans 4-6; Hebrews 9-10: 1-18), through Christ we have an assurance of eternal life. Christ obtained an eternal redemption through His blood (Hebrews 9:12, 14-15).

In Hebrews 9:25 it says, "Christ didn't enter heaven to offer Himself again and again, the way the high priest did because He would have to die many times. He has appeared once and for all, to do away with sin by His sacrifice. Verse 28 says, "Christ was sacrificed once to take away the sins of many people and He will appear a second time not to bear our sin, but to bring salvation to all who are waiting for Him; and by that sacrifice we have been made holy once for all" (Hebrew 10:10).

We are holy not because of things that we do, but because of Christ's Presence in us. Before I came to an understanding of total forgiveness in Christ, I was always living in fear; I couldn't even speak in front of people and tell them about Christ. Why? Because I had a fear that I would say something wrong and disobey God and lose my salvation.

I was a Christian who received Christ in a small church in Brooklyn, New York called, "La Mision" (which means "The Mission") in 1977, but I still had a spirit of fear. I would pray and ask God, why I was like this? I thought other Christians aren't afraid or so I thought. I faced many years of confusion in trying to attain a level of holiness and perfection which Christ had already won for me at the cross (Romans 4 and 5).

Many of you know what I'm talking about. You may be at the point in your life that you're ready to give up because you're so burdened and depressed in trying to measure up and be like Jesus. We're not supposed to be Jesus, but we're washed in His blood. I was trying to reach up to God in heaven, to find peace and joy, but just like in Gen. 11, in the Tower of Babel, this only leads to confusion and hopelessness in our walk and work for God. Yet we neglect Him and His promises. Salvation is to be God reaching down to us to provide a way for us to live in peace and that was His Son, Jesus Christ.

If we don't rest in God's promises we will always live in fear. We won't understand the loving, merciful nature of God which is love (1 John 4; Romans 5). God has given us the Holy Spirit as a deposit, guaranteeing what is to come and therefore we are always confident. We live by faith, not by sight. All this is from God, who reconciled us to Himself through Christ and gave us the ministry of reconciliation. God was reconciling the world to Himself in Christ, not counting man's sin against Him, and He has given us that same ministry of reconciliation. We therefore are Christ's ambassadors as God. We're making His appeal through us. (2 Cor. 5:5-7, 18-20). We are ambassadors of Good News because we have a seal that can't be broken (Ephesians 1:12-14).

Praise be to God because we have received an eternal life of redemption with Christ in the heavenly realms (Ephesians 1:3; Romans 5:1). That's why we should shout and fight, because the peace and hope Christ has given us through his blood. We should be shouting to all people around us, "This is the life, a life full of joy and peace through Christ, a life that is fulfilled because of His love."

Brothers and sisters in Christ, we have something that the whole world is searching for, let's put our religious laws aside and allow the Holy Spirit to minister to your hearts, so He can set you free from the bondage which the law brings. Christ destroyed the barrier, the dividing wall of hostility by abolishing the law, with its commandments and regulations, with His flesh (Ephesians 2:14-15.) We must do the same, if we are to impact our society for Christ!

CHAPTER TWENTY

<u>DREAMS</u>

Glimpse: When I think of my little brother David, I remember how humble and quiet he was. He never had a lot to say unless spoken to, much like my son. He was very articulate and smart. I'll never forget how much he loved children, especially his nieces and nephews. I was fortunate enough to have him watch my son when he was only 3 years old, as I had to go back to work full-time and he was unemployed at the time. He took such good care of him. David lived with us for a short while, and I am ever so grateful for the time we spent together. Although I miss him dearly, David will live in my heart always and forever until we meet again.

---Agnes (David's sister)

The following pages contain various visions and dreams that David journaled during his time here on earth.

DREAM: OCTOBER 18, 1990

I had another dream, I don't know if it means anything or what it's fully saying; I see thousands of people running in fear, trying to get across a draw bridge that's old and weak. Everybody's running real fast across the bridge because they're scared it will fall.

Then soldiers appear and start taking people hostage. They take them in what appeared to be a room, and they start picking people who will live and who will die. They finally kill a young man with his older brother screaming don't kill him. They wanted the older brother to suffer by killing his younger brother and not him. As soon as they killed him a large army, not Americans, come to help us. They freed the people and many people started running away again. It looked like millions of people in cars, on foot, carriages, horses, etc.

Then my family was going to get together for a gathering for the anniversary of my grandmother's death (it was around 1997), it was dark outside, like the sun had been taken away. It wasn't a regular night. They all gathered together on the 7th floor apartment building. Then I found myself in the lobby of the building, I see a huge army coming again, taking over the building and killing people there and going onto all the floors. They are taking people out, rounding them up and they're killing many of them. Now the people start fighting back and killing some of the soldiers. Death and destruction is everywhere.

Then somehow I find my way back on the 7th floor where my family has gathered, and I could tell they didn't know what was happening. I told them without a thought, "two-hundred million Chinese soldiers," but there were other soldiers as well.

As we were discussing if we could sneak out through the hole (the way), suddenly everything changed and the army was defeated. I don't know, but freedom was gone too. My uncle and I said communism didn't stand; democracy didn't stand; only the Kingdom of God stands now! Man couldn't do it, they tried to set man-made rules, but in the end they couldn't stand against a supernatural enemy. They both fall; only God's Kingdom stood the test of time and stood against the enemy (evil).

DREAMS: JANUARY 16-31, 1989

Jan. 16, 1989 - I am walking and see David Wilkerson and his brother, Don Wilkerson coming toward me and they call me to come towards them. When I reach them David Wilkerson puts his hands on my shoulder and tells me to go on, don't stop, and continue in the ways of the Lord. Don't fall from grace and the will of God. Continue to do what the Lord has put in your heart because it will bring freedom and salvation to many people.

Jan. 17, 1989 – I hear the same message regarding going on with God and start the work He has told me to do, to press on!
Jan. 18, 1989 – While reading a book, I receive the same Word I've been receiving for the past few months.

As I read the book *Prophets and Personal Prophecy*, the Lord ministers to me regarding many things that are changing in me for better. One particular thing stood out because the writer had experienced the same thing I had experienced. The Lord showed me in the spirit and brought to mind what He spoke to me through a brother in the Lord, regarding the trials and attacks which caused me to stop writing. He confirmed it was from God to continue on in what God had spoken to me.

Jan. 18, 1989 – This night, I receive another dream. I'm waiting in line to go to a restroom and someone comes from behind me and puts His hand on my shoulder and tells me to go on; to continue to do what the Holy Spirit has put in my heart and not give up, but to move ahead. I hug Him and shake His hand and thank Him for telling me because no one else has told me.

Then I see a line of people I know in the Lord. They are waiting to go to the restroom and as I'm leaving I hear them saying, "that it's from God, it's God's will for Him to do many things for God and for His glory." When I leave the room where the people were, I end up in a church Parish Hall where my family and people I know are sitting. Then we begin to sing and praise the Lord and I awake from the dream. Many things continue to happen to me that are waking me up and preparing me to know that there is a spiritual war going on in the world and the spirit realm.

These past months have been a constant battleground for me and I was not winning the war. I have felt lonely, hurt, depressed, angry, hopeless, isolated, numb spiritually, emotionally, and physically. I've gone through a lot of changes because of this and it has made me stronger in every way. The Lord is bringing me through his refining fire to cleanse me and mold me to become a mature man of God, afraid of nothing in the world or the spiritual powers of darkness at work against us.

Jan. 31, 1989 - I have another one of my dreams with David Wilkerson, but this time he was alone, he came and sat down with me to talk about God and His word. He also spoke of things I needed to hear, so I could have victory and overcome the lies of the evil one. This is the same message I've been receiving from God for several months now; to go on with God and not be dismayed or afraid, but to have faith in God. In His time He'll bring the victory and fulfillment!

I had four dreams and visions to go and do His will and not give up during my trials and testing even though it may seem hopeless. Three confirmations also were spoken to me with the same message, but in different ways, one from a brother in the Lord through prayer in a study, and the next one from a prophet of God through a book, and the last one from a prophet of God in a dream.

God wants to use us for His glory to do His work in an ungodly world and to be willing to give up everything we hold dear in this world and not be afraid of dying for Him and His work. God wants us to be holy, Godly people and to know that He is a great, awesome, and a victorious God and He is to be worshiped, feared and followed in that way! We have forgotten that He's an almighty and living God that wants us to live and serve Him that way.

We have begun to live the same way the world lives and acts. We watch the same things, we go to the same bars, movies, and places we used to go to when we were not saved. If you can take Jesus with you where you are going then go, but be really honest with yourself because you will only be fooled. Jesus will not stop you from going because we have free choice, but you will reap what you sow. If you reap to the flesh, you reap fleshly things that only bring death. The more you reap to the flesh the more your spiritual eyes are closed and die slowly to God's will and way. That's how you can lose your anointing from God and perish by your own actions. Remember we have to choose who we will serve this day and forever! (Joshua 24:15).

DREAM: DECEMBER 1, 1989

I dreamed about myself trying to help people (family). I had to go through what seemed like a mountain. I had to climb up over it and when I got to the top I couldn't go down the other side I was fearful. I had to come down the same side I came up. I really couldn't help my family all the way because I didn't go through all the way myself because of temptation, fear, and testing that was being hurled against me. I had to overcome. I then found myself in my house and I started to pray for an elderly woman who needed strength to go on. As I prayed for her, I myself was strengthened and was filled with joy and spoke joyous words that told me continue or go on.

Then another woman was shown to me, she was younger, but was sick and could hardly walk. People were saying she's dying. She had become a Christian and was involved in ministry, but because she allowed sin and worldly things in her life, she died at a young age with a diseased ridden body. I then went to the front of the house and three people were looking for my sister. They wanted her to come out and they were angry and loud in action. One man looked like a Muslim with a white hat. They were kicking things and throwing things. The woman said something and that she was a witch and they were evil and that she was coming in. I told her, no you can't come in, this is my house and I own it, if you try and don't leave I'll call the police. She got very loud and angry and tried to put fear in my heart.

My family was on the porch at this time and I said to her Jesus has more power than you and she replied something sarcastically like, "Ah, He does." She then rises up towards me because she thinks she can overcome me, but something deep inside rises within me, a Holy anger and the Spirit of the Lord comes upon me and all fear is gone. She thought I was going to run, but I was overcome by the Spirit. She was now heading backwards towards the door and gate and ran with the two men because she couldn't stand against the mighty name of Jesus.

Jesus was teaching me something about that; if we are standing in faith and following His word we will have victory over the evil in this world. If we are half-hearted believers we won't make it over the mountain and the evil in the world. I then was in the dream, sitting at a table with a friend many years later talking about this, saying that if "we are faithful, God will finish all that His will has for us to complete, for His Glory to be revealed in our lives."

God was teaching me to give up the things of the world and surrender all life, every area, including finances, jobs, trials, weakness, etc.

He has done something wonderful today, teaching me about submission, walking in faith, reading and having that time in the prayer closet, not just talking it, but doing it for my spiritual growth. God was ministering to me all last night as I was reading and studying. I was receiving into my heart and mind spiritual things directly from Him, instead of evil things on television and etc. He was saying to me, all it takes is this, "Just spend time with Me, read My word, study it, put it into your heart and then I will answer you. That's all it takes for you to hear from Me, is it so hard for you to do this? Look at My word and see what I've done for you, look at your life see how I've protected you especially these last weeks and you will know why you must continue to be close to Me. Without Me you will die."

It wasn't the dream that was so important, but the still, small voice of God to my heart. The dream happened afterward, it just confirmed it more clearly. I first went into the Word; that's what spoke clearly to me. I forgot about dreams at this time and just wanted to be close to God and just hear His still, small voice speak to me through His Word by the Holy Spirit and He did. I had given Him my time and didn't waste it on foolish things.

DREAM: NOVEMBER 8, 1989

I had another dream of destruction, sweeping across the cities. I don't know fully, but I do know something's coming. I continue to have these dreams, and the Lord may be is preparing me so that I won't be fearful of what's coming because I've already seen some of it.

Maybe I'm supposed to write a book to warn them of the coming calamities on the world, the rumblings our world is experiencing; the rumblings have begun already in our country, North and South Carolina, Texas, San Francisco, Oakland, Puerto Rico, etc. and in other countries since 1988 –Mexico City, Russia, Tokyo, China, Italy, etc.

(Editor's note: These numbers were written in the margins, not sure what this meant? Thought noteworthy of including.)
100,000
41,000
6,045

In this dream I see the buildings of the city falling and exploding in a ball of fire, smoke and dust, some not all, but it's like a sweeping and sooner or later they all will fall like someone is sweeping. The buildings are falling like dominos, one after another, it's incredible.

Then I'm in my house, saying we have to save because we have to be ready for what's coming, we have to be ready. Then someone comes and gives my father some checks because of what we did in helping them; three checks in all and then they leave. That's what I believe in my Spirit, it will have to be in the last days before Christ appears, we as Christian brothers and sisters will have to help one another when one is in need, just like in the New Testament times. We will not let any of our family (in the Lord) starve, God won't allow it, he'll put it in our hearts by His Spirit to help that family.

DREAM: NOVEMBER 9, 1989

The Berlin Wall has been opened. The East part can now go to the free side (West Berlin) without fear of getting shot or killed. The communist government was letting (people) come to freedom without stopping them or killing them. The border has been opened and they are like one country now. You can see it, Russia, Poland, China, etc., all over, communism is dying and giving birth to a new way, that's when the world leader will come to invite everyone and abolish communism and democracy and he will rule supposedly in peace. We can see it coming already, with anti-Christ getting ready to come to power, and a new unity with all countries, a new age world religion and you can see Jesus coming back soon and prophecy being fulfilled right before our eyes.

DREAMS: OCTOBER 10-12, 1989

I had a dream that was very graphic and strong and puzzled me. I'm playing a game with other people (friends), it's "tag" and we're running and hiding. It's nighttime in the streets, hardly no lights when other people (evil) are trying to get us, so I run into a random house. In the house there's blood everywhere and body parts hung on the walls, in the rooms and the floor. I'm running through the house and I run back outside because something is chasing me, so I decide to go back in. Now part of the house becomes a funeral home and someone is standing there in front of me and tells me to go this way and I go, but it's the same there with blood and bodies as well. As I run through a room and then a bathroom, trying to hide, a huge man (it looks like a man) breaks the door and tries to get me, but I run and close the other door and run outside again.

Then I go into the house again, but I go to the same room that I went to the first time. It's downstairs in what seemed to be a basement, but it's a house with dead bodies everywhere and blood and parts of people everywhere, I run outside and some huge woman grabs me and tells me and the other people I was being bad. My friends were scared and we started to run. I said, "Yes I have been bad to you, I'm sorry" and run, and wake up. I have the same dream the next day about the dead bodies and the blood running, but not the end part about the woman.

I then have an even stranger dream, the next day; I'm running into what seems like a huge room, like a prison room. I go in, I get thrown into the room by someone. I then see bodies of animals, people and there is blood and bones all over the room. I'm shocked and scared, then I see something like a dog, he's snarling at me like he's going to attack me. I'm on the floor getting up, then as I get close to him, he starts to get up, but he has blood and looks like he only has bones left on his body and no flesh, but only blood. He opens his mouth and it's like hollow and shaped strange. You can only see his boney insides and blood. He then falls down to the floor like a dog does when he's tired, and turns his face. I then get up and I'm not afraid, but look around and pick up a bone and look at all the bodies in this place and get up.

DREAM: JANUARY 10, 1991

I had another dream of a great earthquake. I was in a stadium when the quake began, and everyone started running and knocking each other down. People were falling everywhere.

When I got outside the walls started to crack and they collapsed onto the people. I looked again and saw the ocean with a huge boat in it that looked like a huge ferry. It began to toss back and forth in the water, and it was like a toy because the water was so powerful in moving it. It then turned over and sank as people were falling over, screaming and drowning. Then I looked again and many people, a number too big to count were standing in a great big line between the stadium and the ocean as they are to be called by an unseen voice; a majestic, powerful voice, and then I woke up from the dream.

CHAPTER TWENTY-ONE
VISIONS AND PROPECIES

David was instrumental in guiding me to the fact that I was in need of a Savior. His relationship with the Lord caused me to search myself and see what was missing and long for a change from the inside out. In 1996 I became a Christian and began attending The Promise Keeper's Meetings and the Men's Meeting at our church and I began growing in my relationship with the Lord.

Sadly, David passed away later that same year. His passing was very difficult for all of us, it still stings my heart even nineteen years later. However, I can find peace in the knowledge that his legacy will be passed on through our families and future generations. I am forever thankful that God brought him into my life and because of him, my life will never be the same!
-- Mark, David's Brother-in-law

VISION: RECORDED DECEMBER 19 AND 20, 1988

It's been almost two years since I had this vision. It was an incredible vivid picture of destruction, but not the way we think of destruction because I believe this will happen in the not-too-distant future.

It has taken a long time to know what it meant because of two reasons: God's will and my disobedient heart to God's will. He tells you things to do, but sometimes you don't' do them, or just put them aside. Well the past 14 days I've been praying to the Lord in the prayer closet, and in my spirit also. I've started my studies on prophecy again. I had been neglecting my studies on prophecy.

I've been neglecting my studies and my time with God and things were not going well in my life. I've had to learn the hard way that you reap what you sow. When you reap to the spirit you reap spiritual things from God. When you reap to the flesh you die to spiritual things and reap fleshly and evil things. When you reap to the spirit it doesn't mean you won't be tested, tried and tempted, but God will enable you to overcome in Jesus name and you will have joy to praise Him no matter what because you have been faithful to him and his commands.

PROPHETIC DREAMS AND VISIONS OF END-TIMES: 1980-1989

In the Summer of 1980 I had my first dream about end times that I can remember. I dreamt that the world was ending, that someone had dropped what must have been a nuclear bomb because the whole world was being swallowed up in fire. My sisters were saying David hurry up and repent before it's too late, before Jesus comes and the whole area we lived in and our house was burning up and then everything went on fire and Christ came to get his people.

In the summer of 1985 I was going to St. Peter's Lutheran Church, and the Lord showed me the scriptures of 1st and 2nd Thessalonians while I was sick for three days. I couldn't even get up from bed because I would get dizzy and fall back in. I've seen Jesus body coming in a cloud and in His hands was the Bible and he showed me 1st and 2nd Thess., so I could read them. I didn't see His face, only His white robe and His nailed scarred hands. After the dream I was able to get up and go to the church prayer meeting and share the dream. The sickness left me after three days.

1985: A vision of the church and its state of deadness as a dirty, defeated place and transformed into a holy, clean, beautiful place (crystal, clean, shining, and radiant).

The vision showed me an old dirty building that at first was like a funeral home, but then when I started looking around I found the people in the church sanctuary on the pews and the floor kneeling down praying, but the prayers weren't being answered or they were not from the heart. The people just stood there defeated, dirty in their state of deadness in that building, no impact to society with the Gospel. Then I was taken to a building that was huge and it was in the heavens hidden in the clouds or surround them, it was beyond description. It was a holy, beautiful, clean, shining, and, radiant place. It was made of beautiful gems gleaming in beautiful radiant light colors, like diamonds. I was taken away from that place. The scripture reference that speaks about being in a radiant, holy and clean place is Ephesians. 5:27.

Around 1986 I had another dream about the tribulation coming upon all Christians. I see myself witnessing in the streets to people and having underground churches because of all the sufferings that the body of Christ was undergoing. I see how we would communicate in that time; we would use handwritten letters like the apostles use and have someone deliver them to their other underground churches. I see myself and others I knew put in prison and many of us were tortured. I also see some witness to the guards and some coming to Christ. I see animals in the prison, like lions, tigers. Then I was taken out and I awake.

I have had dreams of demons coming against me to kill me, but in Jesus name they were put to flight and left me. I've had dreams with a snake trying to overcome me, but the snake got cut off and trampled in Jesus name (Genesis 3:15; Luke 10:19; Romans 16:20). I have also had dreams of going away from a dark fog that was trying to destroy me, but being brought out of that into a beautiful light of peace.

I've had many more dreams about the end of the world, but the one in 1986 is the most vivid of the end of the world as I was taken in the spirit to different parts of the cities of the world to see the destruction.

In 1987 on September 11, while we were doing Bible Studies in Brooklyn at Tony's house, that week they brought a girl who was involved in Spiritism. I had dreamt of evil men trying to kill me or spirits coming with false tongues, to instill fear and trying to confuse me, trying to stop God's word from going forth. September 13, 15, 16, and 17, I had the same type of dreams with demon cults and snakes and also with that girl that came to the Bible study, trying to temp and kill me. I rebuked her...

Jan. 31, 1989 I had a dream with David Wilkerson. He came to talk to me about the state of the body of Christ.

PROPHETIC WRITINGS

Jeremiah 19:1-15
From over the North Pole the deadly missiles will come. Fear and some kind of supernatural impulse will cause the enemy to make the first strike. They themselves will be terrorized by the destruction and havoc unleashed upon the earth. Isa. 23:9, 11, Zephaniah 3:8.

America will never fight against Israel, nor will we protect her. God will protect Israel and send fire on us! If you cannot believe that fiery judgment is near, you must believe it is inevitable. Zephaniah provides it! Zephaniah 3:8

The prophet Isaiah puts it all beyond argument. If you believe God's word is true, then you must believe He is going to utterly empty and spoil any land God judges. Isaiah 24:3

They were warned God would make useless their weapons of war and all their armaments couldn't save them from God's wrath. Jer.emiah 21:4

God said to them, I myself will fight against you! This is an outright warning to America. Jeremiah. 21:5

This is why there will be no retaliatory strikes from this nation or its allies because of the suddenness and finality of it all, we will "forebear to fight" and our missiles will remain in their hold. Our might will fail us in the hour of judgment. Our allies will "become as women" and surrender immediately. Jeremiah. 51:30

God is going to shake all that can be shaken. He is going to shiver into pieces all we once held sacred and dear to us. He is going to judge this nation with such severity; it will cause the ears of all nations to tingle. Jer. 19:8.

God himself will fight against this nation and where he once desired for us only good, how he will plan for us only evil because of the hardness of our hearts (Jeremiah 51); our wound like Israel's is incurable now. (Jeremiah 30:12, 13).

No astrologer, no prognosticator can stop the judgment coming. They may mock and sneer, but they too will burn. (Isa. 47:13, 14) Russia invades Israel because the American eagle is no longer there to defend her. The defense of Israel will not be our battle, but the Lord's, so that Israel will give all Glory to Him. Eze. 39:2, 4 and Eze. 38:22, 23.

This poem below was found under David's bed after his death. It might have been the last thing written before the Lord called him home.

"A Day of Peace"

How good and pleasant it is
When brothers live together
In peace and unity.
No more hurting, no more pain
No more hating and nobody's
a bane…..

March 1996

David Chaluisan, Jr

CONCLUSION

Our Dad never saw David's work in book form, at least not here on Earth, but I'm sure the Lord opened up the heaven's long enough for Dad and David to snatch a Glimpse.

July 9, 2005 began as a day of celebration as a family wedding would soon begin. My husband and I had arrived the day before from visiting his mother in Puerto Rico. The week prior to the wedding, my sister Cindy announced she was expecting her third child to dad and the immediate family. We were ecstatic and filled with anticipation in welcoming a new baby into the family.

It had been a long time since a new baby had entered the family. The youngest of the grandchildren was Analisa, and she was 11-years-old at the time. Dad and mom were so excited, his grandchildren were his world and they felt the same way about their Papa. Dad lovingly referred to them as his "redeemed hoodlums;" his Brooklyn accent made it even more comical to them.

As we were driving to the catering hall, I received a call from my niece Julie that Dad had collapsed in front of the catering hall and was taken to a nearby hospital. Praying all the way, we drove straight to the hospital and found Becky, Julie, and Mom waiting to hear of Dad's condition.

Dad had suffered a massive heart attack, but we were able to see him and pray with him. He did not look as bad as we had expected. He was not well, we could tell, but fully conscious and speaking with us slowly. The doctors were not saying anything.

We left Mom with him, and at about 1:30am, my husband heard a "Code Blue" over the PA system and ran to see what was going on. We did not imagine it was Dad until we saw Mom and she told us dad was throwing up and they asked her to leave the room. Minutes later, they asked us to go to the chapel where someone would come to speak to us.

As we sat in the Chapel, the Lord showed me a vision of dad being escorted by what appeared to be a large figure as Dad waved goodbye. I sprang to my feet and ran through the doors and told the nurse I knew Dad was gone and demanded to see him. She led me to this room and warned me that it was not good. There lay my dad, my hero, on a stretcher and he was gone. Heartbreak is not descriptive enough to express the pain of knowing that a couple minutes prior you were speaking to him and now he's lying there, lifeless.

Suddenly my husband, who had been looking for me, entered the room and just broke down alongside of Dad. Quickly the family started trickling in from the wedding. It was surreal how the room was filled with the people Dad loved the most and who loved him as well.

In the midst, I could sense God's presence and the vision he had given me just moments before. It was a glimpse of glory and a reminder that Dad was with His Savior and that same Savior was their alongside of us in that hospital room. That glimpse of Dad sustained me then and even now. God is so good. In the midst of the darkest day you could imagine, He is there!

Those present were so thankful to be given the opportunity to spend those last hours with him. Sadly, my sisters, Agnes and Marina were out of the state and Cindy was going through a high risk pregnancy, so we were waiting to see if Dad would be admitted to notify her, thus ensuring her that he would recover. Sadly, she arrived after he had passed.

When she was told, she collapsed into my hands; our hearts broke a million times that very dark night. As the evening continued to spiral out of control, I remember crying out, "Oh God, please help us, this can't be happening to us." Minutes later, Mom collapsed when she realized that dad was truly gone. She was then admitted to the emergency room.

So here we were, once again holding on to God for strength and wondering if we would lose mom, as well. This scenario was sadly too familiar to us. As my sisters Cindy, Becky, my niece Julie, my husband, and I gathered around Mom, we refocused our attention on getting her through this horrible night so we could deal with what lay ahead.

Thankfully, Mom recovered, but sadly had to come to grips with the realization that Dad was gone. I will never forget the look in her eyes of confusion and despair. I never want to see that look of utter brokenness in my Mother's eyes again.

A week after Dad's funeral, my sister Cindy lost the baby, and our grief was multiplied. Only now, in retrospect, we can say that the baby was now with Papa and Uncle David and one day, we too would reunite. For now we grieve, but one day we will know God's sovereign hand even in this!

Our family has since had the opportunity to welcome new members into our Chaluisan clan: grandchildren, great grandchildren, and spouses. When David and later Dad were called home, all his girls felt orphaned from male spiritual leadership within the family unit, but God is so faithful and is restoring our broken hearts and filling it with hope and giving us the strength that could only be found in knowing Him.

He is a compassionate and a very present and loving heavenly Father and reminds us of the grand reunion that awaits us in heaven. He has demonstrated to us that our perceived weakness is made strong in Him -- Chaluisan Strong – only in Him!

In closing, I leave you with the following words, the words Dad closed every conversation with his girls, "Don't ever let go of God's hand, Mami!"

Job: 1:21 "He gives and take away; Blessed be the Name of the Lord!"

ONE LAST GLIMPSE

Up until David was born I had four girls. The doctors told me I couldn't have any boys because there was something wrong. I was always praying to God to have a boy, and my dream was for him to be a pastor. Then, God gave me that miracle because I had that boy for 28 years.

Of those 28 years he was away from me for two after we moved to Florida. During that time David stayed behind to enter into ministry. He was studying in New York and had never told me. When I found out, I was so proud and happy, almost crying because God gave me my wish. I said, 'That's a miracle David'.

He then moved to Florida with us, and was working so hard out here in the factory. I never knew of his battles with rheumatism. Yet David was walking and going out and never said anything about the pain. God always gave him strength to do it.

The day he passed away he was supposed to work, but beforehand kept coming in and out of his room like he was waiting for something. I told him I was going to cook before he left, so he went in the room to sleep.

I was sitting down and the house was so calm. You couldn't hear anything it was so quiet. Becky was in bed and I was sitting down in the living room. There was just something happening where we couldn't get up. I finally got up and saw David had not come out, so I went and knocked on the door. When I went in and saw him there, I knew he passed away.

After we called the ambulance, my husband then had a heart attack and we had to run him to the hospital. It was a real mess.

Then the pastor and his wife came from church and she said, "Over here you just come in, and you feel that spirit. There's a peace that you have in this house," and I believe that peace was my son.

David had the same type of heart attack that took my brother at only 27-years-old. They died the same way. But I always thank God because if things are going to happen, they are going to happen. It's His will, not ours.

Shortly after David died I had a dream, and I saw him in heaven. He said to me, "Don't worry mom, I'm with Jesus."

I thank God all the time because I got to have my son. God took him but I know he's in a better place. He was a good boy, and I think he was an angel here.

I didn't know David was writing a book, so now I thank God that I get to be a part of it. I hope that when everybody reads the book it makes them want to follow the Lord, because He's the only hope we have. It's everything we need. We don't need anybody else. Don't wait until it's too late to repent.

-- David's mother

New Year's Eve

Oh, where have you gone?
The time rolls on.
The years fly by.
Another New Year's Eve comes and goes.
Yet here we are, still striving to get it right.
Father Time takes his toll.,
and we must pay its toll.
The older the wiser, that I hope
But we'll still follow history,
For that is how we always go.

We repeat the mistakes of the past,
Oh, how I wish that wasn't so.
For another New Year's Eve comes and goes.

David Chaluisan, Jr.
1/1/96 at 12:24 am

PHOTOGRAPHS

The Early Years: Mom and Dad

ABOVE: Dad holding his first and only son, David. He was so proud of his boy.

BELOW: David with his sisters. From left: Becky, Aggie, Annie, Marina and Cindy. Strong ties forever!

ABOVE: Birthday boy with a beautiful face.

BELOW: Mom and Dad posing with David. They loved spending time together.

ABOVE: David with his cousin Danny, acting as church bat boys.

BELOW: He was truly in heaven in Cooperstown.Here he is posing with his nephew Joshua and a shot of his favorite Met, Tom Seaver.

ABOVE: Mom with her boy, they truly adored each other. No surprise, David has a book, notebook and pen in hand.

BELOW: Another memorable Cooperstown outing with his cousins, Danny and Raphael, and his uncle Juan.

ABOVE:Tossing the ball in front of our old house in Brooklyn. David truly loved all sports.

BELOW: Celebrating his ordination in Staten Island at Cindy's home. He was beaming!

ABOVE: David at Cooperstown with his posse: Dan Jr., Joshua, Justin and Nicky, his nephews.

BELOW: Reverend David Chaluisan, Jr., posing with his younger sister, Becky.

ABOVE: David's nieces and nephews posing with their Grandmother, David's mom, at Justin's wedding in 2013.

BELOW: David's sisters and brothers-in-law posing for a family shot at Justin's wedding.

ABOVE: Dad and some of his siblings along with his own dad; fond memories of our time together.

BELOW: David's paternal grandparents in Puerto Rico, before they relocated to New York.

ABOVE: David on the day of his baptism.

BELOW: David's grave site in Florida, as photographed by his sister, Becky.

ABOVE: David doing what he was born to do, sharing his heart for Jesus during a sermon.

ABOVE: Artwork by David's mother.

If this book has touched your life, you too can have a relationship with Jesus by simply asking Him into your heart.

ACKNOWLEDGEMENTS

As a family we humbly acknowledge our Lord Jesus for His faithfulness, strength and guidance. He has ordered our steps throughout this nineteen year journey; His timing is matchless when we obey. He provided the title, format and aligned all the key players to introduce the reader to Reverend David Chaluisan, Jr. Thank you for entrusting us with David's work and we pray you are glorified with this book!

This family project was a joint collaboration and would not be possible without the contributions, perseverance, encouragement and prayers of some amazing folks and I'd like to express my sincere gratitude to them:

My amazing sisters- Cindy, Becky, Marina and Agnes, my brother-in law-Mark, my cousins Danny and Raphael, my niece Julie, nephew Justin and my children, Danny, Jr., Joshua and Nicholas. Thank you for your heartfelt glimpses and your creative expressions with the book cover. Love you always!

Mom and Dad, you are the anchors and the voice in my head reminding me to bring David's vision to fruition. Your reliance on Jesus is your strength and will remain your legacy. Love you forever Papito and Mommy!

My husband, Danny and my boys, Danny Jr., Joshua and Nicholas for being my sounding board, you encouraged me to read one more page, wipe one more tear, refocus, and push through to the end. Love you more than you'll ever know!

Candice Weiss for understanding the vision for the book cover and putting the pen to paper and illustrating the vision perfectly. Love you!

Justin and Mary Sarachik for assisting from the beginning to the final stages of proofreading and insight were invaluable and introducing us to an amazing young lady that would bring us closer to our vision. Love you both!

Special thanks to Kathryn Sarcone for seeing the vision for the book and your dedication in proofreading, formatting and the attention you give to every single detail that made this book a reality. Your goal setting, patience, and continuous guidance were invaluable and you will always hold a special place in our family's heart! You are a Godsend, love you and God bless!

Thank you to my prayer warriors who cried with me, encouraged me and prayed me through until the end, you know who you are! Love you always!

To my beloved brother David, you have been my constant compass, despite the realms of distance between us. Thank you for allowing me to come along for the ride. I will love you forever and look forward to our reunion and maybe, just maybe, the Lord peeled back the heavens for a brief moment to allow you a glimpse of your book.

--- Anna and The Chaluisan Family

"Every great book is written in the author's blood."

-- Anonymous

Made in the USA
Middletown, DE
10 March 2017